SPIRIT OF THE FENS
A View of Fenland Life
Past and Present

Illustrated by
Sue Scullard

EDWARD STOREY

Spirit of the Fens

A View of Fenland Life
Past and Present

ROBERT HALE · LONDON

First published in Great Britain 1985

Robert Hale Limited
Clerkenwell House
Clerkenwell Green
London EC1

Storey, Edward
Spirit of the Fens: a view of fenland life
past and present.
1. Fens (England)—Description and travel
I. Title
914.26′04858 DA670.F33

ISBN 0 7090 2283 2

Photoset in Palatino by Kelly Typesetting Limited
Printed in Great Britain by
St Edmundsbury Press
Bury St Edmunds, Suffolk
Bound by W.B.C. Bookbinders Limited

Contents

Foreword by Graham Swift

Some while ago I began a novel, *Waterland,* in which, though I did not know it then, the landscape of the English Fens was to play a major part. Since the novel was published I have been often asked why, as an ignorant and perhaps presumptuous Londoner, I chose to write about a part of the country with which I have no personal connection. The short answer, which is far from the whole answer, is that one has to set a novel somewhere and I chose the Fens because of their apparent unobtrusiveness—a flat and empty stage on which to set the drama of my book. This, as I learnt, was merely theory. The Fens, once one's imagination has got to grips with them, are neither flat nor empty, nor are they to be consigned to the passive role of 'stage'. They have a character and drama of their own. What I discovered—and my novelistic encounter with the region was very much one of discovery—was that the Fens, while as richly English as any other part of England, are also compellingly and hauntingly *strange*: they offer the novelist the opportunity to look at his own country and its mentality as one might look at something enigmatic and unknown. It is remarkable that in the 1980s there should still exist in the middle of England a region which most English people find, I believe, when first visiting it, peculiarly foreign; and this elusive and paradoxical quality—when so many other distinctive (and remoter) areas of Britain have been ingested into the nation's cultural and literary heritage—remains for me the central fascination of the Fens. They are both empty and brimming, both cultivated and tenaciously wild, apparently 'open' and 'obvious' yet profoundly mysterious; both solid and liquid, both palpable and mirage-like and ethereal.

My own physical researches while writing my novel were in fact not so extensive. I have never been, yet, to Wisbech or Crowland or Prickwillow. As a writer of fiction I am interested in imagined worlds, and I would much rather hazard an inspired guess at some point of authenticity than go for documentary proof. Yet this very attempt to 'imagine' the Fens has its special logic, for, as the pages of Edward Storey's book abundantly show, the Fens are, peculiarly, not just a landscape but a state of mind, a mood, a human as well as geographical condition.

I could indeed have wished for such a book as this beside me as I made my own independent and faltering investigations of the region. *Spirit of the Fens* is the summation of, though, one hopes, not the very last word upon, a lifelong acquaintance with the Fens by a man who loves them dearly and has already written much about them. Quite rightly, it does not aim at comprehensiveness or exhaustiveness. It is individual, footloose, even quirky. Above all, it illustrates the point which is perhaps especially true of the Fens, that a landscape is the product of its people just as people themselves are shaped by the land. So readers will find here as much of anecdote and reminiscence and sudden glimpses into character as they will of spirit of the place. And they will be entertained, and sometimes moved, as they are informed. I could have wished for such a guide as Mr Storey during my Fenland explorations, but then the best guides are as companionable after, as during the journey.

G.S.

for
ANGELA

By the same author

Portrait of the Fen Country
The Solitary Landscape
Four Seasons in Three Countries
Call it a Summer Country
A Right to Song

Poetry
North Bank Night
A Man in Winter
The Dark Music
A Slant of Light

Acknowledgements

All the people, conversations, places and incidents in this book are authentic, and I would like to express my gratitude to everyone who has contributed in any way. In particular I would like to thank those people who agreed to be interviewed and who gave several hours of their time in answering my questions. Their names are all given in the pages which follow.

For permission to use specific quotations from copyright material I am grateful to the following authors and publishers or agents: John Bennett for *The Fenland Ark*; Ronald Blythe for the paragraph from his Introduction to *The Sceptred Isle* by James Turner; John Calder Ltd., for Margiad Evans's *Autobiography*; Hamish Hamilton Ltd., for L. P. Hartley's *The Brickfield*; A. D. Peters and Co., for Hilaire Belloc's *Hills and the Sea*; Anthony Sheil Associates for F. S. Smythe's *Spirit of the Hills*; the Vicar of Downham-in-the-Isle (Rev. John Hodder) and the Very Reverend William Patterson, Dean of Ely Cathedral, for *The Village and the Church*.

Certain episodes in this book originally appeared in shorter versions in *Cambridgeshire Pride*, and I wish to thank Alex Gordon (editor) and the East Midland Allied Press for permission to use that material for this volume.

The experience recorded in Chapter 7, *Voyage into the Interior*, was made possible by the National Geographic Society, USA, and I am grateful to the Society and Jonathan Tourtellot for allowing me to include an account of that week, which was part of a longer essay written for them.

My thanks are also due to Trevor Hold, Dr Stanley Vann and Dr Arthur Wills for advice concerning the chapter 'Music in the Fens', also to Miss Audrey Fenney, Dr Peter

Cave and Mr Steve Wesley for helping to make some chapters possible.

My wife, Angela, read the proofs; my sister-in-law, Janet, did the typing, and the rest of my family and friends badgered me to 'get on with it'. I am responsible for what is left.

Introduction

'Landscape', wrote Ronald Blythe, 'is among the most potent of the influences which form and govern us. We begin, simply and involuntarily, by taking it as part of the indigenous nourishment at hand when we enter the world, and we eventually need and accept it as a philosophy.'

For me that essential nourishment has always come from the mysterious and elusive landscape of the Fens. For more than fifty years I have been influenced by its great distances, its skies, fields, rivers, places and people. But there is something more than space or light, something more than the weather or seasons. There is history as well as geography. A landscape records also the events and actions of the people who have helped to make it what it is. There is a certain spirit about a place which makes it different from all other places, which gives it an identity and, in turn, draws from its local inhabitants a loyalty which is hard to define.

A few months ago a friend asked, 'Would you ever want to write another book about the Fens?'—implying, perhaps, that I had already written too many and that my furrow had now become a rut. I am sure that at the time my answer was an uncertain, 'No, I don't think I do.' But, a day or so later, I knew that I had not been honest with him, or myself. I did want to write another book about the Fens, but this time it would be different. It would not be just another geography, history or typically topographical book. I wanted to write about the people as well as the places and, through them, try to establish whether there was such a thing as 'the spirit of the Fens'.

But, you may ask, are people born and bred in the Fens all that different from people who 'enter the world' in Yorkshire, Kent or Somerset? In many ways they are—and, of course, it works in reverse. We are conditioned by the place of our birth and early upbringing, by the historical associations, the social prejudices, the local traditions and the soil. As Carl Jung believed, 'The nature of the earth itself had a profound influence on the character of the people born and raised on it. . . .' Whether we stay in that place, or leave it, there is, for most of us, an invisible thread which ties us to the scenes of our beginnings.

It is this idea which I propose to follow in this collection of interviews, essays and reflections, letting people of varying ages, and from all walks of life, speak about what the Fens mean to them. Several of those people were already in their eighties when I talked to them, and their experiences had a certain authority which I found reassuring and exciting. The place and the people belong to each other and, in most cases, are inseparable.

So where do you begin to find this 'spirit' of the Fens? Is there a special area where it can be found, or a particular season? From where do you start, or for what quality do you look if you are to recognize any difference or uniqueness?

I am tempted to say that you cannot find it, it has to find you. It comes when least expected and will appear to different people in different ways. Some may never feel or appreciate it at all, and are excluded from that remarkable spell it casts on others. All the people I talked with (sometimes for many hours) had their own definition of what it means, and their explanations were as varied as their experiences. Others could not explain. As my artist friend Doreen Allen said, 'the Fens is a feeling!'

The prospect of writing another book was not without its problems. Having written three volumes (and several articles) on the subject, how could I begin again and still say something new? There was hardly any area which I had not explored before, and most of the region's roads had been travelled many times. But, as I have proved to myself in the past, it is always the unexpected moment which makes the day, and unless you put yourself in the way of adventure, adventure never happens.

So I set out, to look up old friends and to make new ones. To ask questions and to listen to the voices of older people as well as to nature. There is no particular pattern of seasons in what follows. The book was started in February and finished in October. Sometimes the narrative crosses the boundaries of the year in order to make comparisons, and sometimes a conversation will disturb the chronology in recalling memories of other times.

In considering my task, I was very aware of what F. S. Smythe said in the Introduction to his book *The Spirit of the Hills*: 'Words at their best can only reveal a quality; they cannot do more than present a glimmering of the spiritual truths underlying Man's relationship with the Universe. . . . The task of translating into words more than a tithe of its beauty becomes impossible.'

Here, then, is my tithe, and all I can do in these words is to persuade others that there is a special beauty to be found in the Fen country, a spirit which can be felt by all who are willing to surrender to its particular qualities and to a history which may never be repeated.

You walk the roof of the world here.
Only the clouds are higher
And they are not permanent.
Trees are too distant for the wind to reach
And mountains hide below the horizon.
The wind labours through reeds
As though they were the final barrier.
Houses and farms cling like crustations
To the black hull of the earth.
Here, you must walk with yourself,
Or share the spirits of forgotten ages.

One last word, before the book itself begins. Inevitably there will be contradictions in the pages which follow. The many people I interviewed did not all agree on such controversial issues as stubble-burning, the Common Market, conservation and urban expansion. Some wanted changes, others did not. Some regretted the passing of old values, others saw value only in what is new. It was at least a healthy sign that they were still prepared to sit and talk and air their views, unafraid of being different, unfashionable or argumentative. At the end of the day I don't think anyone had lost a friend or earned a black eye, even though the battle of words was often furious and close to massacre.

In company, or alone, one is conscious of a great richness in the air and of a profound presence which, when found, can never be dismissed, ignored or lost.

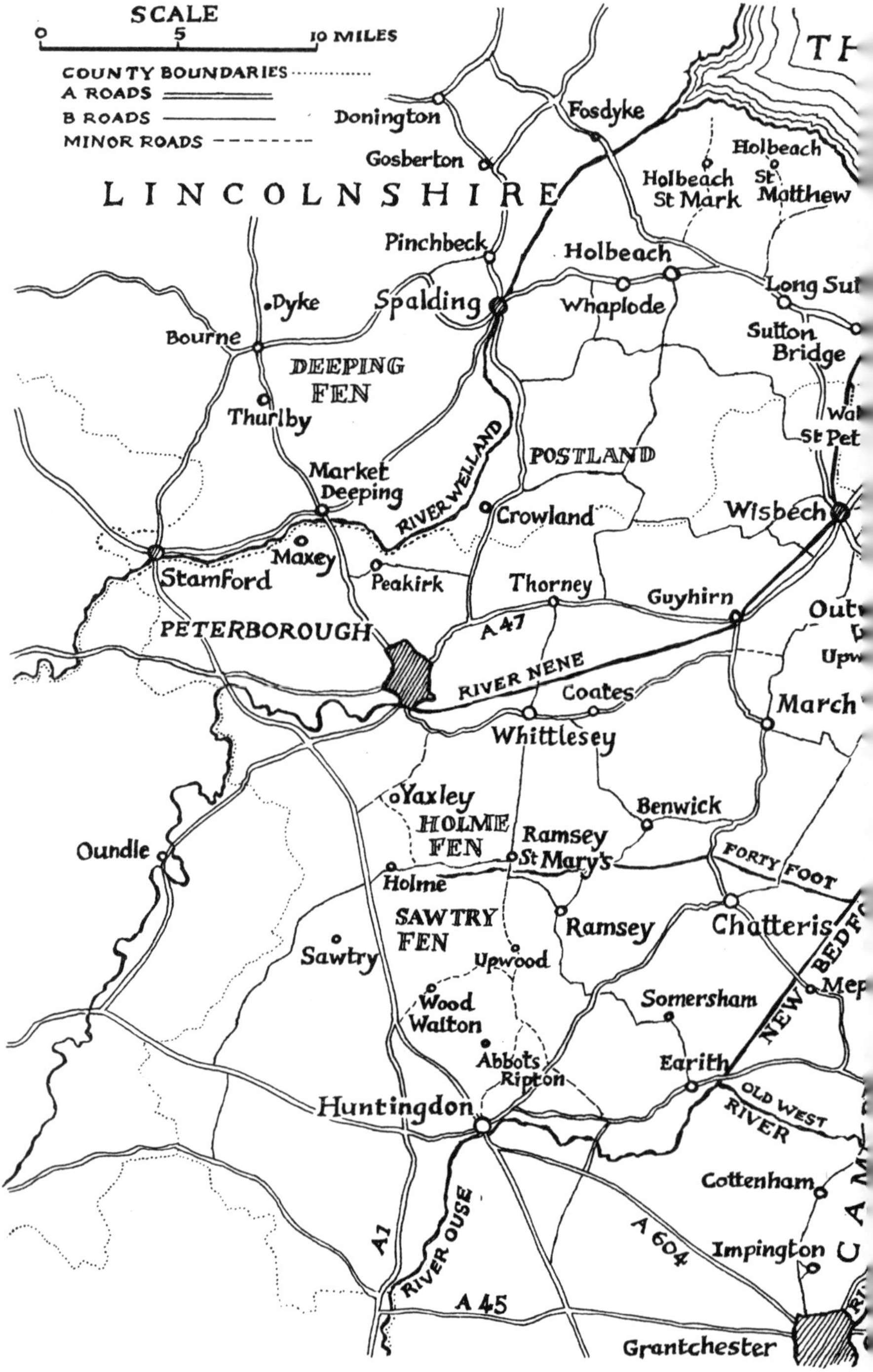

SCALE
0
5
10 MILES
COUNTY BOUNDARIES
A ROADS
B ROADS
MINOR ROADS
LINCOLNSHIRE
Donington
Gosberton
Fosdyke
Holbeach St Mark
Holbeach St Matthew
Pinchbeck
Holbeach
Spalding
Whaplode
Dyke
Bourne
DEEPING FEN
Thurlby
Sutton Bridge
POSTLAND
Market Deeping
RIVER WELLAND
Crowland
Wisbech
Stamford
Maxey
Peakirk
Thorney
Guyhirn
PETERBOROUGH
A 47
RIVER NENE
Coates
Whittlesey
March
Yaxley
HOLME FEN
Benwick
Oundle
Ramsey St Mary's
FORTY FOOT
Holme
SAWTRY FEN
Ramsey
Chatteris
Sawtry
Upwood
Wood Walton
Somersham
Abbots Ripton
Earith
Huntingdon
OLD WEST RIVER
Cottenham
A1
RIVER OUSE
A 604
Impington
A 45
Grantchester

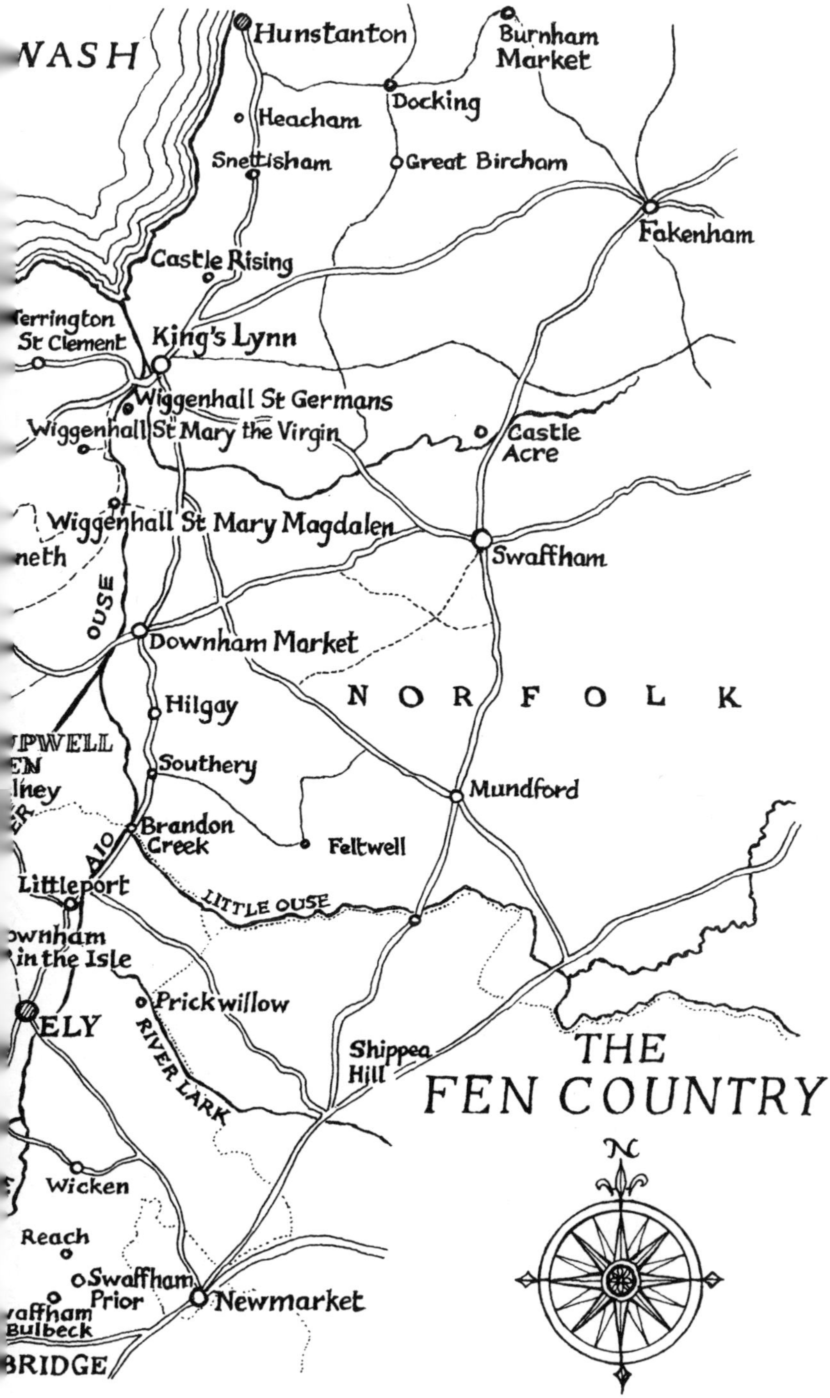

WASH
Hunstanton
Burnham
Market
Docking
Heacham
Snettisham
Great Bircham
Fakenham
Castle Rising
Terrington
St Clement
King's Lynn
Wiggenhall St Germans
Wiggenhall St Mary the Virgin
Castle
Acre
Wiggenhall St Mary Magdalen
neth
Swaffham
OUSE
Downham Market
NORFOLK
Hilgay
PWELL
EN
lney
Southery
Mundford
Brandon
Creek
Feltwell
A10
Littleport
LITTLE OUSE
ownham
in the Isle
Prickwillow
ELY
RIVER LARK
Shippea
Hill
THE
FEN COUNTRY
N
Wicken
Reach
Swaffham
Prior
Newmarket
vaffham
Bulbeck
BRIDGE

1 Figure in a Landscape

I always find it difficult to make a beginning, to take the first step or commit the first word to the page. Having decided that I did want to write another book about the Fens, I sat at my desk and stared vacantly at the wall in front of me. After almost an hour the mind (and the page) remained mockingly empty.

Eventually I knew that there was only one thing to do. I had to leave the comfort of my room, get out to where I could smell the earth, and wait hopefully for something to happen.

February is not the best month in which to undertake such a journey. It is a moody month which can either prolong winter with its grey days and last-minute snowfalls or suddenly pull out of its hat a day which can deceive even the birds into thinking we have skipped a few weeks.

As I drove through Whittlesey towards Benwick and Doddington, I wondered if I had chosen the right route for the occasion. It was all so familiar. Those places had been written about before. So what was I looking for, and where could it be found?

In my brief anxiety I had already forgotten what I had said about not being able to find the spirit of the Fens, that it had to come to me. How easy it is to theorize. At that moment I lacked the faith to believe that anything unpremeditated could happen to me on such an unpromising morning.

When I had driven beyond Sixteen Foot Drain, I parked the car and walked along a narrow dyke-side. Although there was an icy wind coming from the north, there was more than a rumour of spring in the air. Larks were already rehearsing their song, and the day could easily have changed places with one from the middle of April. The air was sharp and clean after the heavy skies of a week earlier.

Then I noticed the water in the dyke. It still looked full of winter, as if its skin of ice could re-set at any moment and drive us back a month.

To contradict that impression, the sun suddenly shone through the dry reeds, giving them a golden sheen more often seen in autumn. It was as if nature was trying to re-awaken all my responses to the seasons in one day, trying, perhaps, to restore my faith.

I found myself surrounded by fields—black, rich, expansive and oozing with history. I could see no one else in the entire landscape. I was alone, and the only dialogue I would have was with the land and its ancient ghosts. Not far away I could see the long, straight banks of the Old Bedford River and a few roof-tops in Welney. In the distance a local diesel train slid along the horizon like an inch of mercury in a mile-long thermometer. The rest was silence—apart, that is, from the ecstatic larks and the eaves-dropping wind shuffling through the reeds.

The persistent wind reminded me that it was far too early in the year to be hoodwinked into believing those warmer days had already arrived. After a few minutes I could feel it penetrating my duffel coat and would not have been surprised to find that I had walked off-course to within a stone's throw of the Antarctic Circle.

As it was, I could hardly move even a few steps. The spirit of the earth would not let me move too far. I had to stand and absorb all the feelings, messages and sensations which the land had to offer. It was as if my feet had taken root in the soil. To have moved would have been to walk away from it all, to reject and lose it.

With an overwhelming sense of gratitude, I realized that if the spirit of the Fens was anywhere it was there, at that moment and in that place. The fields shone in anticipation of the spring. The light vibrated, extending the distances, enlarging the sky. And I, who had witnessed these qualities so often before, felt myself excited again by the way they could still affect me.

On such a morning I am sure that spirit could have been felt anywhere in the Fens, in Hilgay or Marshland, Forty Foot or Postland, for it has many faces, many ways of making its presence felt, and you can never mistake it,

A winter willow tree before pollarding

whatever form it might take. The one thing which is certain is that you can never confine the spirit of the Fens within hedgerows or stone walls—not that we now have many of the one or any of the other. It speaks with the voice of a wind which has travelled many miles. It stares at you with eyes which cannot be shaded.

Although at times like these the Fen country appears (within its pattern of seasons) to be reassuringly changeless, I had to acknowledge that it is, like every other part of the country, slowly being changed both by nature and by Man. It is not the same Fen country that is remembered by many of the people in this book, nor will the Fens which I write about now be the same in another fifty years time. Just as drainage has changed the geography of the Fens, so have machines. Just as we have used the land for our purposes today, so will future generations do with it what they think best. There may be more trees, there may be fewer. Perhaps the hedgerows will be restored, or perhaps the farmlands will become even bigger and more prairie-like. Conservationists may influence the policies made by committees, or we may bequeath to the future no more than a huge, outdoor laboratory where experiments are made in food production but little is left of nature that is ours. The argument, in some ways, is only just beginning. Nor are the dragons all on one side and the St Georges on the other. Selfishness is matched by fanaticism, pig-headedness by resentment. There is both good and harm being done, and we are not the ones who will necessarily reap the rewards of our actions now.

Slowly I began to see what it was I wanted to say in the book which was still to be written. I wanted to preserve as much of what was left, simply for others to enjoy. I wanted to record the thoughts and feelings of people who had known the Fens longer than I, and I wanted to extol more clearly the qualities of a landscape which is so often misunderstood.

Feeling that I had just made a New Year's resolution, I made my way back to the car to begin what I thought would be my journey home. But, just as I'd had no strength to move my feet on the dyke-side an hour earlier, so now I felt as if I had no power to direct the car in the way I wanted it to go. It was as if the magnetic fields had been changed and all the compass-needles now pulled south. Involuntarily I let the steering-wheel turn in the opposite direction to the one I should have gone. The spirit of the Fens, it seemed, was not letting me escape that easily, whatever my plans.

I gave in. The day was now too good to spend cooped up in a room answering letters or pounding a recalcitrant typewriter. Those tasks could be done when it rained or when fretful clouds sulked in a sky that had forgotten how to sing. Instead of forcing myself to go home, I had to follow the 'call of the wild' and travel whichever way my invisible navigator wanted me to go.

Experience has taught me that from such impulsive decisions unusual discoveries are made. I had to trust my instinct to lead me into the path of adventure. Somewhere there was a place I had not visited before, or a person I had not met. The past had only been a preparation for the present. The land was both familiar and unfamiliar, the roads travelled and untravelled. I felt as if I had just arrived and yet, in some strange way, had been there before in some previous existence. I threw out my arms to embrace the day. I shouted joyfully at the sky. I felt the engines of my inner being suddenly switch on and the rhythmic pumping through the veins begin.

Knowing a little of Fenland history does help one to appreciate and make sense of the landscape. I was aware of this as I drove from Manea towards Welches Dam. The fields were not just there for the sake of being there, nor had they always been in evidence. They were the work of man and had been won out of many years of conflict with the elements. The rivers and dykes were not always part of the landscape but had been dug out of the marshes and wilderness which had once covered most of Cambridgeshire. They were the evidence of struggle. Every field, bridge, tree, house and church had its own history. Everything the eye can see is there for a reason. Flood, famine, hard work and survival are written in the fields.

As I walked along the banks of the Old Bedford River, I thought how easy it is sometimes for the imagination to witness again all those dramas when they are played back on the vast screen of sky, or on the enormous stage of the fields themselves. I was but a figure in a landscape. Before me was a pageant of turmoil, tragedy, comedy and achievement that no theatre could hold. By the end of the day, and a hundred miles later, I knew why I felt the need to write 'another book' about the Fens.

When I returned home, I looked at the Ordnance Survey Map to retrace my unpremeditated journey. The names of all the fields and places I had seen danced like a child's skipping song through my mind:

Eastrea, Coates, Eldernell and Goosetree;
White Moor, Bedlam, Binnismoor and Franks;
Laddus, Upwell, Nordelph and Barroway;
Denver, Hilgay and Ten Mile Bank.

Benwick, Wimblington, Chatteris and Ramsey,
Ranson, Benson, Latches Fen and Stow;
Mepal, Welney, Welches Dam and Manea,
Coveney, Pymoor, Fodders Fen and Mow.

Ely, Littleport, Shippea Hill and Feltwell,
Southery, Burnt House and Brandon Creek,
Popham's, Pingles, Jenny Gray's and Horsemoor—
All true Fenmen have black-webbed feet.

And is that all you can produce, I ask myself, after a day out? Well, that and a few other ideas which will eventually help to fill up all those empty pages which frightened me so at the beginning of the day. Feeling that I still needed some consolation, I savoured the words written by Henry David Thoreau on 31 March 1845: 'The really efficient labourer will be found not to crowd his day with work, but will saunter to his task surrounded by a wide halo of ease and leisure. . . . Those who work much do not work hard.'

That made me feel much better. I will try to work hard, leaving 'a wide margin to life', and, if I let it, something will surely happen.

2 Return Journey

Time and time again the Orcadian poet Edwin Muir, who is now buried in Swaffham Prior churchyard, wrote of the need to return, to 'Seek the beginnings, learn from whence you came/And know the various earth of which you are made.'

With that advice in mind, I go back to where, for me, this lifelong love-affair with the Fens began, to the town of Whittlesey, which was then in the Isle of Ely. The word 'isle' appealed to me even as a child and gave me a sense of independence. We were different. I liked the idea of being an 'islander', someone separated from the mainland and the usual affairs of men. I was not sure what it meant or why we were on 'an island' but I thought it sounded right. I was convinced that when the day came for me to leave my home town I would have to go by boat.

This impression was not without historical foundation. The Isle of Ely had, indeed, once been an island, as had Whittlesey, Ramsey, Thorney, Welney and most other villages in the Fens before drainage began to change the features of the landscape. I can remember several times during my childhood when our town was cut off from its neighbours, when flood-water lapped at the parish boundaries with a gnawing persistence, and men had to be rowed to work in small boats instead of going by horse and cart. I would sit mesmerized in the tiny kitchen of our house and listen to stories of river-banks bursting, of storms, floods, blizzards and fires. There was always an element of drama even in the simplest of lives. Nature was not something which one just admired. It was something against which one fought. This daily conflict with the old adversary went a long way towards shaping the character of the people as well as their land. People and events came before places then. I felt that I belonged to a particular breed of men long before I became aware of my own feelings about the countryside around me.

The spelling of Whittle*sey* and Whittle*sea* must not confuse: it is optional. The suffix *ey* or *ea* simply confirms that the town was once an island which belonged to a Saxon landowner by the name of Witle (or Wyttel). We have never been able to agree on which spelling to use. The railway station had one and the post office the other, and although the *sey* is more commonly used now, there are many of us who would feel saddened if the *sea* disappeared completely.

Looking through some old newspapers the other day, I came across an account in February 1901 which said that, 'Whittlesey, the largest parish in England with a population of between 7,000 and 8,000 people, had not reported one case of drunkenness during the whole year. It once had a very different reputation but now was one of the most sober districts in the Isle.'

I smiled at that, for its reputation for hard drinking certainly survived well into the thirties, and, with fifty-two pubs to support, it could not have been easy for the locals to live up to those new claims of sobriety. There were five pubs in the street where I was born, but I have to admit that as a child I did not see much drunkenness. There were always the usual two or three neighbours who rolled home, not quite knowing where home was, but they did not make me feel that I was living in a town of iniquity.

I did not think the town could ever excite the imagination of anyone other than a native, but a recent experience proved me wrong. People born there always remain loyal to it wherever they may eventually live. I have heard from men and women who left forty or fifty years ago, who still speak of it with affection. Such allegiance is to be expected. But when a 'foreigner'—a man from another part of England—is bowled over by it, then I have to start thinking about the old place all over again. Although my fondness for the town, with all its associations, has not changed, it was, perhaps, timely that I met an 'outsider' who was to re-awaken the old fascination and memories.

The moment which sent me back to considering again the

character of Whittlesey (which is only six miles away from where I live now) was a conversation with the North Country poet Pete Morgan, who was on a week's working visit to Peterborough City Libraries. Like Edmund Blunden sixty years earlier, he could not find suitable accommodation in that city and chose to risk the untried hospitality of my home town. Anyone could do worse. In 1920 Edmund Blunden had found refuge in a pub called the Queen's Head where, as he recalled in his book *The Face of England*, 'We were led along the flagged passage, up twisting staircases to some garrets, all beams and shadows.' The floor had hollows in it, and the palliasses had fleas in them. The landlady told him that she would not have the undertaking of him as regards food, and the landlord, 'who had grown almost the shape and colour of a pollard willow', spent most of his time telling his young guest strange stories of the Fens.

The Queen's Head was just one of the many pubs out of the fifty-two which was to disappear under the dust of the bulldozer, hidden now (and perhaps appropriately) under the town's new public library. It would have been too much of a coincidence if a poet of today had chosen to shelter beneath its sagging roof. Instead, Pete Morgan stayed at the Boat Inn, at the end of the street where 'I entered the world', at the edge of the town before it surrenders to the open Fens of Cambridgeshire.

Like Mr Blunden, Mr Morgan was enthralled by the place and its characters. 'By, they certainly know their local history', he said, 'and they know how to enjoy a few pints. The whole atmosphere of the place just bowled me over. I really must come back one day to take a closer look and hear a few more of those amazing stories . . .'

At that moment I told myself it was time to go back, back to the old hunting-grounds before someone else took over my patch and wrote about things I had not yet discovered. After all, Pete had found out that the Boat Inn was haunted, which was something I did not know, and, furthermore, it was haunted by the ghost of someone who had died when falling into the river from Briggate Bridge. But who?

I have crossed that bridge thousands of times but have never thought of tragedy. It has always represented for me years of happiness and contentment. It was the bridge by which I crossed out of the ordinariness of our street into that world of nature which I knew as a child. It was a landmark, a gateway into freedom. When I reached that bridge and walked a little way along the riverside, I was able to enjoy the smell of fields and water, to delight in the great open spaces of the countryside, which I did not know then as 'the Fens'.

As a child I did not understand the meaning of such geography and had no idea why the world at the end of my street was so flat, magnetic, spacious and free. I took the immense skies and far distances for granted, concerning myself more with those things closer to hand—wild flowers in a grass verge, birds' nests in hawthorn hedges and that modest stream we called 'Briggate River' or 'Creasey's Bank'.

It was, I discovered later, a tributary of the Old River Nene called 'King's Dyke'—after King Canute—and it flowed as a liquid boundary round the town from Whittlesey to Peterborough. My grandmother had been known to skate its seven or eight miles to the city in winters I had not known but only heard about round the Christmas fires.

Briggate river—or 'Whittlesey Dyke' as I should have called it—flowed in the opposite direction to join up again with the original course of the Old Nene at Flood's Ferry before flowing on to March, Outwell and Wisbech, finally reaching the Wash. But, as a child, the only River Nene I knew of was the big river which flowed from Peterborough to Guyhirn, on the western edge of the town, and the little river where I played and fished was known always—at least by me—as 'the Briggate'. To change its identity now would be to take from it an element of its fascination.

My own memories of the river are always of summer. It was my favourite stretch of water in a land where waterways are as common as roads. When I was a child, my mother had taken me for walks along its thickly overgrown banks, and I had paddled in a clearing where the gravel bed moved like golden pebbles under my feet and a shoal of minnows sniffed around my ankles. Sometimes I would make reedboats and launch them downstream in the hope that they would somehow reach the sea. A few yards away my ambitious armada would keel over in the wind and limp forlornly into a congested harbour of bulrushes and moorhens.

It was a curving stream where I pretended to fish with a home-made rod and some bread bait, a stream where I first ventured alone as I grew older and wanted to explore that enormous landscape for myself. As I sat among the tall grasses and cow-parsley, I looked across the water to the church of St Andrew, almost hidden by a cluster of chestnut trees. That church marked the end of our street, apart from Briggate River, and I knew that beyond it was *my* town, *my* world, all that mattered and all I thought I would ever need. To my left the familiar brickyard chimneys squeezed their lazy smoke on to a pure sky, and behind me the Fens stretched away into the beginning and end of Time. Skylarks sang interminably, dozens of them frantically trilling away in such frenzy that I thought sometimes they must surely burst or explode into stars and burn themselves out in space.

If that river, fishing and skylarks can transport me back to those days of more than forty years ago, so too can wild irises. My riverside was adorned like some royal thorough-

'Brickyard chimneys squeezed their lazy smoke on to a pure sky'

fare for a jubilee. But fortunately no crowds came, no noisy bands disturbed the soft music of the wind through the reeds. The yellow flags waved only to acknowledge the passing of a dragonfly or to give visible proof of the wind's existence. The irises were more than just bright yellow—they too were golden. I remember picking some once and taking them home for my mother, who was ill in bed. As I entered our tiny house, the flowers seemed to light up the room. They spoke of warmth, summer, the freedom of the river, and fresh air. Above all, they were more beautiful than any flowers I could have purchased at the florist's, even if I'd then had the money with which to buy them. I put them in an empty pickle-jar and watched them glow in the deepening shadows of the house. I could not wait until tomorrow and the chance of walking again that path by the water. It was mine. I felt that even the grass and birds were beginning to know me.

Behind the river and the railway line which ran close by was the Fen country itself. Miles and miles of uninterrupted space and rich, black farmland extending beyond the boundary of the eye towards a horizon which shimmered like a thread of heat at the edge of the world. There earth and sky met, or seemed to meet. Between them was some mysterious chasm in which the clouds grew and from where the sun and moon rose in their appointed time.

Gradually, from the conversations I heard at home, those fields began to have names—Black Bush, Underwood's, Flag Fen and Glassmoor. On the other side of the town towards the Wash there were the chiming names of Delph Dyke, Bassenhally and Moreton's Leam, all names associated with aspects of the history which had gone towards the making of the Fens. I still did not understand the origins or the magnetism of that landscape even then. Only now can I look back and see that most of what I have written about during the last few years has its roots in that soil, in the land worked by my ancestors.

It was only later that I began to learn something of those earlier settlers—the Romans, Anglo-Saxons, Danes, Normans and Dutch who helped to fashion this land for those of us who were still to come. The very name we gave our river—'Briggate'—was of Scandinavian origin. King

Canute, Hereward the Wake, Cornelius Vermuyden and Oliver Cromwell were no more than names to me in those tattered history textbooks at our school; books used by our parents who had been taught by the teachers who now taught us. I did not know of the part these famous men had played in the history of my own landscape as I sat by the water, staring at the fish who were staring at me. I saw only the heraldic display of the river-bank with its dandelions, buttercups and irises.

It is only in recent years that I have tried to understand the meaning of belonging to a place, of having roots in a certain area where one feels most comfortably and naturally at home. In the beginning I wrote only for the joy of writing and for celebrating nature where no one could hear me. It did not occur to me then that this countryside was different, that my poems might be recording a small part of its history as the farm-labourers and their daily tasks were gradually being taken over by the machine. It was only when I started writing my topographical books that I began to examine this relationship between a man and his landscape. Is the 'spirit of place' I used to ask, something we create for our own needs, projecting our feelings into the landscape making *it* accept us rather than *we* accept it? Or does the landscape itself have a spirit which we learn to recognize, absorb and draw from until, in the end, we are shaped by the very nature of the soil from which we come?

As I have already explained, I found the answer in the words of Carl Jung, who believed that people do become expressions of the soil. The characters I subsequently came to know, and write about, were to confirm this view. I also realized that I was lucky enough to be part of a long (and, until recently, largely unwritten) tradition. The people I met, and the people I had known all my life, were expressions of the soil, especially those who had lived and worked in the Fens all their lives. They had a philosophy about the land and spoke of it as one would speak of a living animal. It breathed. Each field had its own character, its own independence.

When I am talking with Fenmen, I notice that far-distant look in their eyes, that quiet but belligerent response to life that has known all the vicissitudes of nature, the cruel winters and the beneficent summers, the winds, floods, seasons and harvests which they have helped to control and conquer, creating a world which we can now enjoy and appreciate. Whether they are working with animals or machines, they are an extension of the land, a living evidence of what Jung claimed. They are an integral part of the soil, just as the soil is part of them. Their behaviour and their attitudes are conditioned by it and, hopefully, always will be.

Since I began writing about the Fens, much has changed, sometimes for the better, sometimes not. Land and farm buildings which were a feature of the landscape just ten years ago have already disappeared. Quiet lanes have become busy roads, minor roads have become dual-carriageways (a quaint term which overseas visitors find amusing). Farm machinery now costs four or five times what it did, and the value of land has reached prices which, for our grandparents, would have bought half the country. East Anglia has also become a fashionable place in which to live, and the old-established communities are losing something of their traditional identity. Even when I go back to my home town, I feel I need to buy a new street-map in order to find my way around. So much has changed.

As I look back now to that earlier world, I have to agree that I must have changed a little with the experiences which have since crossed my own narrow path. But, inescapably, I have to admit that I am still essentially that child who walked by that river, and my physical response to the land around me is just the same as it was more than forty years ago.

3 Through Other Eyes

Since I wrote my book *The Solitary Landscape* in 1975, the North Bank road of the River Nene between Peterborough and Whittlesey has, unfortunately, become a very popular route, as busy almost as the main road. I would not like to be thought conceited enough to assume that my praise of it then has been in any way responsible for its appeal now. The increased volume of traffic on all our roads, and the speed with which most people like to get between one place and another, has inevitably meant that alternative routes have been sought. The North Bank road was just too convenient to be ignored for long.

When, as a boy, I first knew the road, it was little more than a track on which you could have a bumpy bike ride. Now it has a good surface and provides a straight, fast approach to the city, or a quick escape from it. Only at rare moments of the day can I recapture some of the spacious solitude which I wrote about in my earlier volume, and it might be unwise or indiscreet to say now when those moments are.

I still travel along the North Bank as often as ever before, and I am fortunate in being able to do so outside the local rush-hours. To the north the low fields unroll towards Thorney and Lincolnshire, to those Fens which have a totally different character and atmosphere from the Cambridgeshire Fens. To the south I can look over the Washlands and the outskirts of my home town of Whittlesey, which was once held within the prominent landmarks of our two parish churches—St Mary's and St Andrew's. The town has outgrown those boundaries now, and the life I knew then belongs to another era. As L. P. Hartley says at the beginning of *The Go-Between*, 'The past is a foreign country . . .', and my childhood in that town now feels as if it belongs not only to another time but to another place.

Something which I did not know as a child was that the writer L. P. Hartley was also born in Whittlesey. Admittedly he did not stay there very long, no more than five years, but he did write about it (and the surrounding Fens) and can justly be claimed as one of the town's sons.

I first met L. P. Hartley in the spring of 1964, during the John Clare Centenary celebrations which were being held in Peterborough. He was by then a highly acclaimed and successful man of letters, more in love with Venice, London and Bath than Whittlesey, the author of more than a dozen novels, many short stories and countless reviews. He had just published a novel called *The Brickfield,* and that in itself intrigued me. Having spent all my childhood in Whittlesey under the constant pall of smoke from brickyard chimneys, and having visited my father many times at the King's Dyke kilns, where he worked as a burner, I was puzzled to learn that anyone could write a novel about them. It turned out to be not so much a story about brick-burners and brickyards as about farmers and early love. The disused brickfield in the novel was only the setting for a more sinister drama and was near Crowland, not Whittlesey. But my curiosity was aroused and I looked forward to meeting the author. As it happened, I was to be present at a private and personal moment which was not witnessed by anyone else.

The major literary attraction of the Clare Centenary was to be a lecture by Edmund Blunden, who had recently returned to England after his many years in the Far East, particularly in Tokyo and Hong Kong. He was now living in Long Melford and, not being a driver, wanted overnight accommodation in Peterborough. As L. P. Hartley was in residence that weekend at the family home, Fletton Tower, it was arranged that Edmund Blunden should stay with him.

On the Saturday morning after his lecture Blunden had asked me if he could be taken round the Clare countryside again, which he had not seen since 1924. I called for him at ten o'clock and was shown into the room where the two men had just finished breakfast. These esteemed and

Looking over the washlands towards Whittlesey

ageing writers were in the act of presenting to each other their latest publications—Blunden giving to L. P. Hartley *A Hong Kong House* and Hartley giving to Edmund Blunden *The Brickfield*.

I have to say that I knew more about the poet than I did about the novelist but I promised myself that morning that I would get a copy of *The Brickfield* as soon as possible, to see what it was like. Even though it was not what I expected, I was not disappointed. In any case, I told myself, as the author was born in my own home town I ought to know more about him and his books. The fact that a whole world of difference separated us did not matter. The years, the circumstances and the backgrounds created a gulf which I could not even expect to cross. And what was I to learn?

Leslie Poles Hartley was born in one of the larger houses of the town on 30 December 1895. His father was a solicitor who practised in Peterborough and who had had an interest in the brick industry. He is still remembered as a highly cultured and literate man who was one of the best after-dinner speakers in the area, a gift his son was not to inherit. L. P. Hartley's mother was Mary Elizabeth Thompson, daughter of a Crowland farmer. As a child Hartley did not enjoy good health, and when his mother learned of the open drain system of Whittlesey—where refuse was regularly seen to flow down the streets—she decided that it was not a fit place in which to bring up her son, so the family moved to Peterborough and the mock-Gothic house which is now always associated with them—Fletton Tower. There the child who was to become the well-known author went to the city's grammar school and received music lessons from the cathedral's Master of Music—Doctor Haydn Keeton, a man who had a reputation as a strict disciplinarian and kept an assortment of canes close at hand for the correction of his choristers and music pupils.

Although Hartley was never to be a confessional or autobiographical novelist, many of his childhood experiences and impressions were to find their way into his work, and especially into *The Brickfield*. Some of his descriptions of the Fens, and of Crowland in particular (which in the novel is called Rookland), are memorable. For him the ruined front of the abbey is likened to a beggar holding on his stiff arm a coat with a hole in it, and the author's admiration for 'the sublime half-circle of the dog-tooth arch' is always apparent. There were times when the abbey became 'bluish and misty and insubstantial' and seemed to float in the air—'I saw the frost-eroded forms and haggard faces of the saints and kings whose effigies clung crazily to the wall of the West Front. . . .'

However brief, insubstantial and distant Hartley's love of the Fens became in later life, he retained an ability to evoke the atmosphere of the area as only a native can. He understood the people as well as the land. With a wry, knowing smile the main character in the book Richard Mardick, says, 'the only hills the fenmen knew were the artificial slopes that led to bridges. Between the road and its attendant dykes the grass verges often narrowed, leaving little room for error on the driver's part. . . . You could hardly see the water for the blanket of greenish-yellow scum that grew on it—cott, we called it. A strong wind would sometimes curdle it and pile it up in ridges . . .'

The Fenman's idea of a hill is a familiar joke. The Market Hill of my home town is no more than an inch higher than the rest of the streets but we always talk about 'walking up to the hill'. Several landmarks in the Fens which are known as hills are no more than bubbles in the tarmac on a hot day but we speak as though they were in the Himalayas.

If ever I need confirmation of the unique character of the Cambridgeshire Fens, I have only to look at other landscapes which casual eyes might say are similar and I realize what a totally different feeling one gets in this part of the country. Having experienced the lowlands of Holland and Belgium, having spent some time in other flat areas of England—Romney Marsh, for instance—I am more convinced than ever that the landscape of which I write has something which others lack. Other regions, it is true, have their generous skies, their well-kept farms, their long rivers, reed-beds and exciting sunsets, but the Fens have something more than these often-praised attractions. For me their distances have what I can only call 'nearness' or 'immediacy'—which will sound like a contradiction to anyone who is not a Fenman. There is also an individuality about them which other landscapes lack. They are not remote or aloof, only partly hidden from the undiscerning eye and frightening to those afraid of space or silence. They can be gentle, intimate and welcoming. They can comfort as much as hills or inspire as readily as the sea.

My feelings about the Fens were confirmed a year ago, when my wife and I were staying at a converted oast-house in Kent. Our room was in the tower, or 'roundel' as it is more correctly called, with large windows in the sloping roof which narrowed to the traditional white cowl for which that county is famous. The cone-shaped ceiling was high and timbered, a cross between a Norman hall and a spaceship. The oast-house itself was next to a working farm in the middle of a field, approached by a lane thickly embroidered with cowslips and primroses. We were greeted by a buxom girl, who could have stepped out of the Middle Ages, and shown to our rooms. Lying in bed at night, we looked through uncurtained windows to a sky full of bright stars. It was exciting and, in a child-like way, breath-catching. The spaceship image became a reality as we appeared to glide imperceptibly through the heavens. Immediately above my head was the Plough, balanced on its shaft. Orion was already slipping out of sight, but a million other stars dazzled in the dark which knew no other light imposed upon it by civilization. It was as if the whole world was asleep. But before I joined all those who were, my mind went back through space to those years when, as a boy, I loved nothing better than to walk out at night into the Fens and stare up at the Milky Way, at all the nameless and numberless worlds in the sky above me, and wonder what it all meant. At that moment I longed to be released from my time-capsule, to be back on those familiar roads, alone with the night.

One reason for spending a few days in Kent was to see for ourselves the countryside which H. E. Bates had written about so prolifically and evocatively since his early days in Northamptonshire. Our pilgrimage had the added blessing of an accidental meeting with the author's widow, who kindly showed us round the garden of the house where she now lives, a garden which happily overlooks the one created by her husband. Relating a comment we had received from the village churchwarden that, 'Mr Bates was a great asset to the community', she said, 'oh, I don't know about that. We were just ordinary people, really. My husband liked cricket, gardening and writing. He didn't go to church very often.'

Looking at his adopted county, I could see why it meant so much to him, but where, I ask, do we find his deepest love of the countryside shining through his writings? Surely in his descriptions of Northamptonshire and the Nene Valley, in that green and modest corner of England where he grew up, the place he knew so well as a boy.

We continued on our journey through the hop-gardens and the enchanting villages of Kent, along roadsides as profuse in wild flowers as the lane was to the farm, and then over to that great expanse of Romney Marsh. And there, for a moment, I was reminded again of the Fens. But not for long. The more I looked, the more I knew they were two totally different landscapes.

From Romney we crossed the border into Sussex and the Cinque Port of Rye. The charm of this delightful town was not even diminished by the acquisition of a parking ticket for outstaying our welcome by ten minutes. But within half an hour of being there, I was reminded again of home, because it was in that town that the poet and dramatist John Fletcher was born in 1579. Later, as a boy, he received some of his education at the old grammar school in Peterborough minster precincts when his father became dean of the cathedral. So, try as I might, I could not escape the associations with home, and I found myself thinking not about Rye but about somewhere much closer to the heart.

Perhaps it is necessary to get away from home once in a while to see the familiar through other eyes and to experience again the irresistible pull of knowing that you belong to a place which cannot be supplanted by any other.

As I drove into the minster precincts, I felt that I had come to as near as home can ever be now without inhabiting the past forever.

4 A Modest Conservationist

I had arranged to meet Eric Slote at his house in Ramsey St Mary at 2.15 p.m. but, in my customary anxiety to be punctual, I found myself fifteen minutes early. To delay my arrival, I drove for a short distance along Glassmoor Bank to get a smell of the Fens. It was a cold, raw day for the middle of March. The featureless sky was elephant grey, and if the blurred horizon could have stared back at me with any feeling at all, it would have done so with that misty look you get sometimes from a lizard's eye. It was as if the world was only just beginning and lay there uncertain about what to do next. The low, long fields were empty and lifeless. A dry, primeval wind honed itself on the brittle reeds—a harsh, abrasive sound that only a summer sun would eventually soften. I could have been a skeleton for all that the wind cared. I felt my bones growing fleshless and hurried back to the relative warmth of the car. Surely, I thought, my friend would not mind if I arrived five minutes early.

I first met Eric Slote two years ago when I was the subject of a BBC television programme and we were filming in the Ramsey area. The producer, Mike Purton, wanted a shot of an old ruined windmill, and the only one which seemed suitable was the one at Ramsey St Mary. I did not know then who owned it, but a few questions locally soon put me in touch with Eric and, from that moment, I knew I had met a genuine and enthusiastic Fenman. He could not have been more helpful. In asking to photograph the mill, I soon discovered that he was a keen conservationist and that the three acres surrounding the mill were quietly becoming his own private nature reserve. Weeds and nettles were allowed to grow in profusion so that rare moths and butterflies could find a natural habitat for breeding. Nature was being allowed to take over on a valuable piece of Fen soil because, as Eric explained, 'I felt that I'd spent all my life taking from the Fens and I wanted to put something back before it was too late.' So he bought this special piece of land (and an old disused railway track) to create a wilderness, an island of wildness in a sea of intense cultivation.

Eric's family had farmed in the Fens for at least three generations, and he has worked on the same land for more than fifty years, doing every job there was to be done 'except thacking a straw-stack'. 'I can remember', he said, 'how as a boy I used to go into my father's fields and play with the binder-wheels and how fascinated I was by all the wonderful signs of life around me. Of course in those days there was an abundance of butterflies, bees, insects and birds. The air used to hum all day with the sound, and there were that many skylarks you couldn't count them.'

Within minutes of being in his company I had forgotten the cold world outside and was reminiscing with him about those warmer days of two summers ago. Something which intrigued me then, and which I wanted to hear about again, was how he had re-introduced frogs into this part of the Fens by bringing back jars of frog-spawn from North Wales.

'Well, it happened like this,' Eric patiently explained. 'I was on holiday at the time and I woke up one morning and heard the frogs croaking, and it took my mind back to when I was a boy. Frog-croaking was for me one of the loveliest sounds in the Fens, especially when they were coming up to

Eric Slote's mill and nature reserve at Ramsey St Mary

spawn, and I thought how nice it would be to hear them again. When I told one of the Welsh farmers about this, he said, "Why not take some of our frog-spawn back with you? We have too many of the beggars here.' So, jar by jar, and year by year, Eric brought home from Wales a new supply of spawn to put in his own Fenland dykes and garden pond. 'It was like getting my boyhood back," ' he said with a smile.

With the return of the frogs, you get a return of snakes and water-birds which haven't been seen in the Fens for a generation or more. Understandably there are some species making their homes there that Eric was not keen to talk about, in case the wrong people became interested.

'I want my "island", as you call it, to be the breeding-ground so that all these creatures can be given a chance. Then, with a bit of luck, there will be plenty for everyone to see. In my opinion conservation is more than making a place look nice. It's about creating the right environment for the whole of nature's life-cycle. That's why I think that some of these conservation committees are not always on the right track. It's no good just putting up a couple of big trees here and something else there, just to look pretty or fill a gap. We want thornbushes for the finches and buildings for the barn-owls as well. We need natural wild areas and streams which breed life. The dykes today are too clean sometimes. There's no life in them. Drainage has become too efficient, and the water-tables are often six foot lower than they should be . . . but I mustn't get on to my high horse, otherwise I shall start getting angry.'

Mrs Slote decided that a cup of tea was called for, and I took the opportunity to change the subject to horses. 'Oh yes, I loved working with horses when I was a young man. Ploughing could be one of the most satisfying jobs on the land. I've always loved horses. People used to sing and whistle when they worked then, but you never hear that now. Everything's changed.'

I asked Eric what he thought of today's Fenman. 'All the true Fenmen have gone,' he said. 'They're a different breed today. In the old days there was what I can only call a brotherly spirit among Fenmen which isn't there any more. Everyone was prepared to help one another, and there was always such a good community spirit in the village. We had concert parties, chapel choirs and a cricket team which was made up entirely of men from Ramsey St Mary. We used to play matches against Ramsey Town and Holme, and a good few others. We had some decent players, too. Of course there weren't the cars about then to take people off to Peterborough. When I was a boy, you could play whip-'n'-top out there on the main road all day and hardly see a vehicle. Now you can hardly cross the road without running the risk of being knocked down.'

Out of all Eric's loves I got the feeling that his greatest passion must be for the variety of bird life in the Fens. 'I've been interested in birds all my life and, as a child, I used to watch their flight patterns and study their nesting-habits. When we were working in the fields in them days, you would never disturb a nest if you could help it. Plovers used to nest in the fields then. I remember once, when we were potato-planting, we had an old crawler-tractor which used to pull the planter, and the driver would always lift the planter when he came to a nest, and the eggs would remain unharmed as the tractor tracks passed on each side. The bird would wait until the last minute before flying off and would be back on the nest again by the time we returned on the next run. The poor creatures wouldn't stand a chance now, which is why they've learnt to nest elsewhere. It's the same with skylarks. The only place where they can nest now is on the grass verges, and even they're disappearing. . . . I think one of the most exciting sights in the Fens for me is still the arrival and departure of migrating birds, expecially the golden plover. We wait for them to come and we wait for them to go and at each moment life changes. It's the same with swallows. You could say that the migration of birds is my calendar. They govern my seasons.'

At that moment a tame blackbird in the garden came up and looked in at the window. 'Ah! You'll have to excuse me a minute,' said Eric, 'while I give him his tea. He comes every day and knows he'll always get something.' The blackbird hopped towards the opening door, collected his tea and then hopped back into the garden. 'Do the frogs come, too?' I asked. 'Not yet,' he said, with a smile which suggested that any day they might.

I then asked Eric which part of the day he liked best and,

without hesitation, he said, 'The dawn. I love to be up early and I love to be out at the mill to hear the dawn chorus. You see, I love solitude . . . and silence. The first sounds from the woods or the fields tell you that a new day has begun, and for that I am grateful. And, next to daybreak, I like evening. I often say to my wife, "Do you feel like going out to hear the nightingales?" And we creep off and go to where we know we shan't be disappointed. It's heaven!'

As the grey light of the afternoon faded, I knew that I would soon have to leave that warm room and make my way home. But there was still much to talk about—sticklebacks, eels, lizards, insects with such lovely names as 'water-boatmen', stoats, herons, winters, harvests and the need to introduce more fennel if the swallowtail was to breed successfully, or how willowweed was allowed to spread on land to be drilled with sugar-beet seed, only to be sprayed off once the soil and seeds had been consolidated.

Eric then produced some old postcards of photographs taken in August 1912, when the Fens were flooded and the harvest had to be gathered in by boat. These interested me expecially because in a family Bible which my parents own there is an entry by my grandmother about these floods and how the men had to take to the boats to save the crops. And here were pictures of that event, with the fields flooded as far as the eye could see and the stooks sticking out of the water like the tips of extinct volcanoes.

'One last thought, Eric, before I go. What do the Fens mean to you now?'

'Oh, that's difficult to say. You see, you grow into an area and that area grows into you until, in the end, you can't tell who's boss. I'd miss the Fens, of course . . . the wide open spaces, the sunsets and the birds. . . .'

And he could have added the red admirals, the tortoiseshells, the peacocks and occasionally the swallowtail, not to mention the grebes, the cormorants, otters and a hundred-and-one other things which made up this modest man's peaceable kingdom. 'I feel sorry for the young people of today,' he said quietly. 'They'll never see the things that I have seen.'

It is worth travelling out in any weather to meet someone

like Eric Slote, a man who loves his countryside and all that it has to offer, a man who would say with Thoreau, 'In wildness is the preservation of nature.'

As I drove home, I was reminded of our first meeting, which had led to my writing a poem call 'Roots'. The words of the last verse came back to me as freshly as if they had just been written:

Today I met a man who shares
my fascination with these fields.
He said 'It is not what you see,
it's what you know. Each furrow
is a lifeline on the hand. Each reed
a symbol of our ancestry.' I stand
and in the silence hear again
familiar voices rising from the ground.

So it always will be with men who belong to the soil as much as Eric does.

5 The Word on Water

I first learned of the Fenland Ark from Eric Slote, whose grandmother had gone to her funeral on what used to be called 'the Floating Church'. It sounded such an unusual and fascinating episode of Fenland history that I was curious to find out more.

Coincidentally, within a few weeks, I heard that Holme parish church was to present a festival celebrating the story of 'the Ark' and that a new book by John Bennett was to be published which would give a full and historical account of how the Ark came into being.

Unfortunately, because of commitments which took me away from the Fens for a week, I was unable to attend the festival. I did, however, get a copy of the book and decided that I must track down its author to find out how he had discovered so much about this otherwise forgotten chapter in the church's ministry of eighty years ago.

Months passed before I put my resolution into action but eventually I contacted Mr Bennett and arranged to meet him at his house in Holme. It was a traditional March-leaving-like-a-lion morning, with strong winds buffeting against the mountain ranges of grey clouds. The incredibly black soil of the fields was freckled with countless pieces of carrot, remnants of the unwanted crops which had been ploughed in. I stopped the car to smell the unforgettable smell of those fields and was reminded later of how J. Wentworth Day had once said that this was the only place in the country where you could still smell Saxon England.

From Mr Bennett's exuberant enthusiasm for his subject, I knew he could not be 'local', for people are reluctant to talk so freely about the past to a stranger. It usually takes 'an outsider' to look under a few village stones and find out what has been happening there for a hundred years or more. John and his wife, Brenda, moved from London to the Fens in 1960, and it was through a brief reference on an illustrated map of Huntingdonshire that he first became interested in the Fenland Ark.

'It's been called several things in its time', John explained, 'the Fenland Ark, the Floating Church, even the Tabernacle . . . and when I found out there were still people living in the area who had been baptized on this church, I thought it was worth making a few more inquiries.'

The man who first had the novel idea of taking to the water to reach his flock was the Reverend Horatio George Broke, who became the vicar of Holme in 1895. It was a parish which had grown steadily since the drainage of Whittlesea Mere in 1851 but it was still divided by many waterways, both natural and man-made, and in winter much of it could be under flood. When the new vicar realized that his parishioners were frequently kept from attending church not only by distance but also because the roads were impassable, he decided that he had to find ways of getting to them. With a name like Horatio, what better way than to build a boat and reach them by water? It was, after all, not without precedent.

Towards the end of the nineteenth century, Church leaders throughout the country were becoming increasingly concerned about rapidly declining congregations and encouraged any initiative which might win them back. In some parishes Church Army vans became commonplace as young, evangelical lay officers tried to take the Word to remote areas. But their vans were of little use in the Fens, especially during the winter months, and the Reverend Broke decided that the most effective way of defeating the water was to use it. His parish had at least nine miles of navigable rivers and dykes. With a suitable boat he would be able to get where no other means of transport could. His parishioners could then have no excuse for not attending church. So, out of his own pocket, he set out to get a boat built. His church would become a floating church, the first ever seen in the Fens.

There had always been good boat-builders in the area, and some of the best had their yards at Stanground near

Peterborough. In the autumn of 1896, the Reverend Broke cycled from Holme to Stanground to discuss his ideas with a Mr William Starling. Having listened carefully to the vicar's requirements, Starling said it would cost £35 to build the punt and a further £35 to build the house which was to be 'the church': the equivalent of about £1,000 at today's value.

The vicar justified his ambitious plans by explaining that at least forty-two houses in his parish were two or more miles away from the village church and that many of these were within a mile or less of the river, some practically on the river-banks. It seemed sensible to take the church to the people rather than to expect them to make the effort to get to church.

Although the cost of building the floating church was to be borne by the Broke family, the cost of maintaining it would fall on the parish. Consequently there were those who wondered whether this eccentric idea would be worth the expense. But when the vicar pointed out that, if they did not support him, they would be depriving two hundred less fortunate parishioners of the only chance they would have of attending Holy Communion, there was no further argument.

Throughout the winter months of 1896–7 there were many other problems to worry about if his idea was ever to become a reality. The level of water in the rivers varied dramatically, which meant that the clearance beneath the bridges varied also. The house on the barge had been designed to a height of seven feet, but the clearance at the bridge at Froghall, for instance, was as little as six feet in November. Excessively wet winters would make that part of the proposed route impossible.

Work nevertheless went ahead, and George Broke and his wife became so enthusiastic about their project that they would frequently cycle through the most appalling weather to see how Starling was progressing at Stanground. A deadline had been set for the end of March, as arrangements had already been made for the Archdeacon of Huntingdon to dedicate the new 'church' on 5 April 1897. Starling kept his word, and the boat was delivered to Stokes' Bridge on 1 April. Sadly, as an unfair reward for his labours, fate decided to make the poor man miss his footing on the gang-plank and he fell into the water.

Instead of a bell to call his flock to church, the vicar flew the flags of St Andrew and St George. There was a congregation of about forty people as Archdeacon Vesey blessed the church and dedicated it to St Withburga. Suddenly, from the normally silent waters of the Fens, rose the sound of singing. Mrs Broke accompanied the hymns on a small American organ and, as the people looked at the altar, reading-desk and miniature font, it was clear that they would be able to worship on the boat without any lack of ceremony.

The first normal services were held at Stokes' Bridge on Easter Day, commencing with Holy Communion at 9.30 a.m., at which only four communicants were received. But by four o'clock Evensong the crowd had grown so large that the congregation spilled over onto the banks and heard the service through the open windows.

'It was at that service', said John, 'that the name of Bertie Rootham was entered in the Register of Baptisms as the first person to be baptized not only with water but on the water. Four others were added at the same time, and many more were to follow. In fact, during its 7½ years of ministry, seventy people were baptized, and there are still old residents in the village today who can remember those unique occasions.'

John had planned to take me over the routes which the church used to follow but, with so much to talk about, the four hours of the morning had gone before we knew where we were, and we had to postpone our excursion until another time. I had at least learned from his book that the Fenland Ark was able to reach isolated families in the parishes of Wood Walton, Ramsey St Mary, Ponders Bridge, Farcet and Yaxley, serving 'as much of that part of the Ely Diocese as possible'.

There were four main stations on the Ark's circuit—Stokes' Bridge, Charter Farm, Allen's Engine and Black Ham, the latter eventually being removed from the timetable because of the recurring problems with the bridge at Froghall. The Reverend Broke had written to the Middle Level Drainage Board offering to pay part of the expense of raising the bridge but had received no help. Services were, however, continued at the other three stations unless the weather made it impossible for the church to move. On one occasion it was frozen as solidly into the ice as it would have been in the Arctic Circle.

The novelty of the Fenland Ark caught the imagination of both the local and national Press. During the first six months of its life, illustrated articles appeared in the *Peterborough Advertiser, Hunts Post, Harmsworth Magazine* and *Strand Magazine*. Even 'Boxer', one of the horses used for towing the barge, became something of a celebrity.

In addition to playing the organ, Mrs Broke ran evening classes on the Ark for the girls of the parish, teaching them a few home crafts as well as their weekly portions of scripture. Some of these girls also made up the church choir and would occasionally be invited up to the vicarage for tea as a reward for their services.

Frequent applications were received by the vicar from people who thought it would be romantic to get married on the water but the Ark had no licence for such ceremonies and they had to be content with the more conventional setting of the church in the village.

After the energetic efforts of the vicar and his wife to take the Word into the waterways, as well as the highways and byways of his parish, it must have been a sad day for them when, 7½ years later, their dream came to an end. The floating church was becoming increasingly difficult to maintain, and major repairs meant that it had become a greater burden on the parish finances. The novelty had also worn off and the zeal of the faithful few had diminished. There were times when the vicar had to write in his diary: 'Service at Stokes' Bridge—no one came.'

In the end the Reverend George Broke was forced to admit that the extra work had affected his health and that it would be unwise to go on preaching in such inhospitable conditions. The journeys over the Fens, particularly in winter, had become tiresome and he had begun to feel physically exhausted.

In 1904 it was decided that the floating church could be put to better use in other parts of the diocese and, early in November of that year, it was towed the fourteen miles from Stokes' Bridge to Welches Dam, along the historic waterways of the Old Nene River, Forty Foot and the Old Bedford River, where it was handed over to the Reverend F. G. Guy, vicar of Manea.

I sensed the disappointment in John Bennett's voice when he came to this part of the narrative. 'I couldn't get anywhere in Manea with my inquiries,' he said. 'It was as if I had come to a dead end, like the floating church itself. All the plans they had for it there came to nothing, and two years later the barge was returned to the Reverend Broke as "unwanted". It was in such a dilapidated state that he removed all the furniture and put the boat into dry dock.'

The Fenland Ark never sailed again. It was taken from Ramsey St Mary back to William Starling's yard at Stanground, where it was bought for a few pounds by a group of young men who wished to renovate it as a summer houseboat moored on the Nene near Orton Staunch. They nicknamed it 'The Saints' Rest' and used it for about six years before it finally sank and was broken up for firewood.

'At least, that's one story,' said John. 'There is a belief that it is still buried at the bottom of the Nene. I'm not sure. Perhaps it's right that there should be a bit of a mystery about it, although, after doing so much research, I think I must favour the theory that it was used as a "bungalow" before being broken up for firewood.'

The Reverend George Broke himself retired to Holme Hale Hall, near East Dereham, where he died in 1932. Much of what he worked for, and stood for, has disappeared from the modern life of the Fens, and the floating church has become another fragment of that hidden country which we can so easily forget. But it was a worthwhile mission and a chapter of local history that I was grateful to learn. In producing *The Fenland Ark*, John Bennett has added greatly to the knowledge and pleasure of all who are interested in these links with the past.

'And it's not finished yet,' he said with unflagging enthusiasm. 'I've had dozens of letters from people who can remember the Ark, or had some family connection with it. The diaries of the Reverend Broke are a story in themselves. He was a very elegant writer, and his daily entries give you a marvellous insight into the life of the times.'

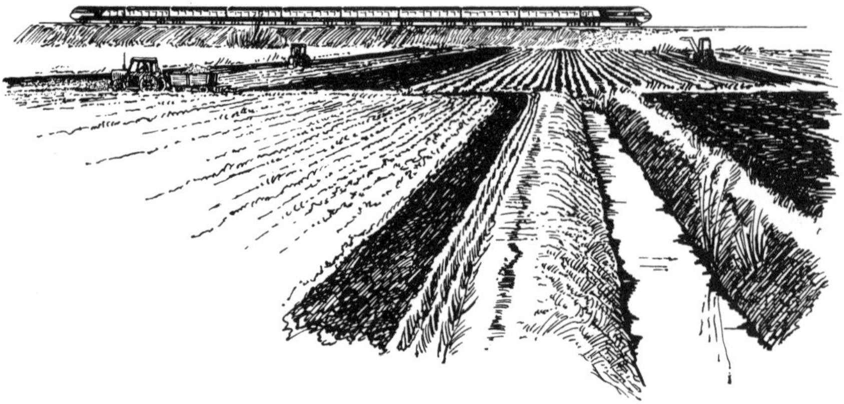

'A high-speed train slides quietly along the horizon at Holme Fen'

I, for one, hope there is more to come, that Mr Bennett will look under a few more stones and discover something from our past.

As I drove home across the Fens, I stopped once more to smell the fields and to take a picture of the black soil of Holme. As I did so, a sleek 125 high-speed train slid quietly along the horizon, pulling my mind back to a very different world from the one I had been in all morning. Perhaps one day even that form of transport will seem as antiquated as the Fenland Ark, and historians will want to know what people did with themselves on those long, tedious journeys between the place of departure and the place of arrival.

6 A Lifetime and a Half

The hourly measures of time are soon forgotten in the company of an eighty-two-year-old man who can recall an extraordinarily busy life with candour, clarity, wisdom and humour. Although I have had many long conversations with Hugh Cave of Thorney, I don't think we have ever covered as many subjects in detail as we did recently, when a whole day sped by quicker than an hour spent at a less interesting task. We ceased to notice the abbey clock chiming off the portions of the day, and by the time darkness arrived we had discussed a thousand years of local history, politics, marriage, religion, travel and, as expected, the building trade.

Hugh's family has been associated with building for 150 years, ever since his great-grandfather started the business in 1830, when the parish of Thorney had a population of two thousand people, forty-five shopkeepers and tradesmen, seven pubs and four toll houses, and sent three thousand sheep a year to the London markets. Before that his ancestors had been in farming for eighty years.

Our marathon day of talking began because I asked a simple question about the construction of pill-boxes during the Second World War. Now the one thing about Hugh Cave which you can be sure about is that he will have a file of papers on almost any topic he wishes to refer to, so his answer to my question was detailed, methodical and illustrated by documents most people would have thrown away after forty years.

In some ways the reply I received became less and less important as the background to the story unfolded, and I sat enthralled as I listened to a chapter of Fenland life which might not otherwise be recorded unless I attempt some recollection of it here. As we move rapidly towards the end of this century, I become increasingly aware of the links we still have with its beginning, especially with the people who were born when the nineteenth century was stepping nervously into the twentieth. During the past few weeks I have talked with several men and women in their eighties, and there are no better history books.

Although Hugh was born in 1902, he is not an old man and never will be. Even a few knocks early in life did not dim his positive attitude to living. His mother died when he was only thirteen months old and he was brought up by some aunts, the memory of whom still makes him smile and shake his head. 'They were tartars', he said, 'and certainly gave me a tougher time than I might have expected as a child.'

After three years at Thorney Infants School he was sent to All Souls' Roman Catholic School in Peterborough, where he stayed until 1918, when he attended Bean's Commercial School in the cathedral precincts for a year's tuition in shorthand, typing and book-keeping. Illness prevented him from taking up a building apprenticeship in Birmingham and so he became a part-time clerk in a local drainage office, which could offer him morning work only. This at least gave him the chance to learn about the building trade and, although work was scarce, he joined his father's business in 1920, earning half-a-crown a week. In his spare time he turned to bee-keeping, gardening and rearing chickens in order to get more pocket money. Four years later his wages had risen to £2 a week, out of which he had to pay half for board-and-lodging and then clothe himself.

'But it wasn't all drudgery,' said Hugh with remembered pleasure. 'We had our good times. There was always something going on locally in those days and we would often have an evening round the piano, singing all the old songs. I went on holiday, too, with some relations in Birmingham who took me to Colwyn Bay and Westcliff-on-Sea. I must say it was marvellous to get away from my Thorney aunts for a few days.'

By 1925 the business was looking prosperous as the family firm won contracts from the Thorney RDC to build ten council houses and also had the job of carrying out extensive alterations to the Rose and Crown. 'But', continued Hugh, 'just when we thought everything was going well, my father died in December 1926, and his brother and partner was, for various reasons, unable to carry on the business. So it was all left to me. I was twenty-four, with very little capital and three aunts to support. Fortunately my father had instructed me in every branch of the business—estimating and supervising, as well as the manual skills, so I was able to keep things going.'

Throughout this leisurely narrative I was shown scores of old photographs, account books, indenture deeds and faded newspaper cuttings. The table and the sofa were weighed down with scrapbooks, and the carpet was littered with letters. Perhaps it was just as well that Hugh's wife Renate (a second marriage), had taken a guest back to Peterborough and was not expected until nearer lunchtime. Not that she would have objected to such chaos. Her own enthusiasm and collections would have just added to it, for she has become as involved in all these subjects as her husband.

In 1928 Hugh decided that the time had come to specialize in concrete constructions and, despite some energetic competition from national companies, gained several important contracts, particularly in drainage, which, as he soon found out, was a branch of the work fraught with difficulties because of flooding. 'And then,' he said with a lighter tone, 'I decided to get married to a young lady I had first met in 1921. The aunts weren't very pleased about it, and there was such a holy row that they refused to attend the same church in Peterborough and, from then on, went to March instead. But I got married all the same and we spent our honeymoon in London at the Regent Palace. When we came home, I had 10 shillings in my pocket and £5 in the bank.'

But a new phase in Hugh's life had opened and, with his usual optimism, he and his first wife moved to a bungalow on the Causeway. 'The early thirties were not easy years and, as you know, there were thousands of men on the dole. But we survived and in 1934 I had the good fortune to win the contract for building the Elwes Hall in Peterborough with a tender of under £5,000. The Hall was built for the Roman Catholic Church and named after the Elwes family who were the major benefactors as well as being related to the Rector of All Souls' Church. The Hall now belongs to Perkins Diesel and is used as a Social and Recreational Centre. At the same time we also won the contract for re-building Thorney Bridge and a new vicarage at Whaplode Drove, so we moved back to the village and lived on the Green.'

By the end of 1938 Hugh, like many people, was convinced that war could not be very far away. 'And, as if we knew that it might be the last Christmas we would all spend together, we decided to have a great family party with relatives and friends staying with us. There were nineteen of us by Christmas Eve. Fortunately in those days the firms we dealt with gave presents at Christmas, and we had received a couple of turkeys and a York ham, which Mr Bristow the local baker baked for us in a rich pastry which I can taste to this day. My wife made a hundred mince-pies and we had fourteen pounds of sausages, Christmas puddings, cakes and fruit galore. I just forget how much bread and drink there was but we had a marvellous time. And then on Boxing Day we all went into Peterborough to see the pantomime.'

There was never to be another Christmas like it. The following year war was declared and life changed for everyone. Labour and materials were needed for other purposes—and it was at this point that we finally got round to the subject I had gone to discuss—pill-boxes.

'We were finishing a shelter at Postland that Sunday morning,' Hugh recalled, 'when the announcement went out on the radio that war had been declared on Germany. Searchlight batteries arrived almost within a matter of hours and I became Leader-Warden of the local A.R.P. Although private building had just about come to a standstill, we were soon getting work from the War Office, on what became known as the Home Defence Line, which meant erecting pill-boxes at strategic sites in the area. I was made Group Contractor for Thorney, Whittlesey, Crowland and Eye and had the authority to organize local firms to carry out whatever work had to be done. The first three pill-boxes were built at Welches Dam near Welney, and we couldn't have had a worse problem to begin with. Because of the state of the river-banks and the nature of the Fen soil, we had to build a light railway to convey all the building-material from the road-head to the site four hundred yards along the bank and then dig down eleven feet for a foundation. In ten days I wore out a brand new pair of very stout shoes and got very little sleep. We worked for thirteen hours a day, seven days a week, for five weeks, and then thankfully went onto normal time.'

'Were all the pill-boxes of the same design?' I asked.

'No, they varied, depending on the nature of the site they were supposed to defend. GHQ had three basic designs. One was for an anti-tank pill-box which carried a six-pound naval gun and bren-chamber, then there was a smaller box for a bren-chamber and rifles, and one for rifles only. The walls were two feet six inches thick, made up of an inner brick wall and an outer brick wall with reinforced concrete poured in between. Then of course they were camouflaged.'

I asked Hugh how many of the boxes he was reponsible for, and he told me twenty-five. "There should have been more but the new general who took over the command of Home Defence insisted that all his forces should be mobile, so the War Office cancelled any plans it had for further constructions. There were, of course, many more built because the local county councils erected their own to defend important crossroads and bridges. I think I'm right in saying that there were four thousand built throughout the country between June and December of 1940—and not one of them was used, at least not for the purpose they were intended . . . but that's another story.'

The war also brought to Thorney a prisoner-of-war camp to accommodate twelve hundred German prisoners, who built their own theatre from scrap material dumped by the Americans. They formed their own drama group, choir and orchestra, and, as the war progressed and the bitterness receded, the prisoners entertained their captors at their camp concerts.

I was hoping to see some photographs of this episode of Thorney's history but had to be reminded that there was no film available for private photography during the war years.

And so the hours passed. Towards the end of the war, fired with a determination to work for his community, Hugh went into local politics and became actively engaged in county council committee work. In 1944 he was co-opted onto the Isle of Ely County Council and during the next thirteen years served as either Vice-Chairman or Chairman of Thorney RDC. He was also a Justice of the Peace for Whittlesey and President of the Peterborough Builders Association.

But there were to be set-backs. In 1952 his wife died on St Valentine's Day, and his own health began to deteriorate so that he was forced to retire temporarily from public life. Fourteen years later, however, an unexpected romance led to his second marriage in 1966 to Renate, an endearing and still vivacious lady from Hamburg. The story of their meeting, and of their life since, is a book in itself. Renate has adopted the English way of life so completely that she knows more about our customs than we do.

One day when I visited them she had specially prepared a favourite dish of beef stew and Norfolk dumplings. In the centre of the table was a small vase of snowdrops which she had picked from the churchyard. When I raised a questioning eyebrow at this, she said, 'It is quite all right. I had a word with the Lord. "Dear Lord," I said, "I am quite sure you would much rather have a few of your lovely little flowers in my warm house than out here in the cold churchyard, wouldn't you?" And He said yes!'

Like Hugh, Renate has been involved in the community, with 'Meals on Wheels' and the Women's Institute, and during the summer months she occasionally serves as a guide in Peterborough Cathedral. Music, painting, literature and visiting English country houses help to keep her as young as her husband.

In 1973, at the age of seventy-one, Hugh decided, with renewed enthusiasm, to take up committee appointments again with both Peterborough and Thorney councils. So far he has given over twenty-four years of his life to the needs of his parish and its surrounding communities. Despite heart surgery and two pace-makers, he is still chairman of the parish council as well as treasurer and booking-agent of the Bedford Hall.

'In the centre of the table a small vase of snowdrops'

The imaginative conversion of the nineteenth-century Tank Yard to the modern and well-equipped Bedford Hall (named after the Duke of Bedford) was the culminating triumph of Hugh's life. During many years of political wrangling and hostility—when the building was almost demolished—Hugh held firmly to his vision that the Tank Yard would one day become the village community centre, catering for banquets, dances, concerts, lectures, exhibitions and local club activities. In April 1981 his dream came true as he cut the tape to declare the new Bedford Hall open. It had cost £60,000 but already has proved a success, with bookings up to two years in advance.

Have all the years of hard work been worth it? 'Yes,' he says. 'To promote a healthy and lively community spirit is always rewarding.' Which is why, no doubt, he also founded the Thorney 'With Great Pleasure' evenings, where local people open their homes once a month to other people who would like to share their interests in music, literature, local history or any other subject which appeals to them—'Like a good old-fashioned evening round the piano,' said Hugh, 'instead of just watching television.'

I stole another look at my watch. I could not let the abbey clock chime midnight again and me still there. There would be other hours, other days to make my way to that house and spend some time in such warm company. For someone who has already lived a lifetime and a half, Hugh takes a very optimistic view of the future and, with an ageless twinkle in his eye, speaks enthusiastically of all the joys that are still to be.

Surrounded as he is by his devoted family of four children (and their children) and a village full of friends who refer to him affectionately as 'Mr Thorney', he intends to make his second pace-maker work hard to earn its keep.

7 Voyage into the Interior

One of the most pleasant surprises to me in 1984 was not that George Orwell's prophecy for that year had failed to come true in England but that there were still so many areas of the Fen country for me to discover.

Through the courtesy of the National Geographic Society of America (for whom I had been commissioned to write a chapter on East Anglia), I was able to hire a boat for a week to explore the Fenland waterways. One of the first things I realized (apart from the fact that even a small boat is a big craft when it's your first experience) was that rivers give you access to those secret places in a landscape which are otherwise inaccessible. Also a boat (however clumsy you make it) allows you to sneak away from the rush and tear of modern traffic and, at a maximum speed of four miles an hour, gives you time to see the world around you. In addition to that pleasure, there is the freedom of being able to 'park' more or less where you please for a reasonable period of time—say thirty hours instead of one.

So, feeling a little more adventurous than usual, I accepted the editor's suggestion and set out in early April to make my maiden voyage of the Fens. Fortunately my wife was free to accompany me, and her parents (who had just arrived from Canada to spend Easter with us) were willing to make up the crew. Our boat was called *Tranquil Waters III*, a consoling name for such an inexperienced party.

Appropriately our voyage began at Earith on a late Saturday afternoon which shattered any ideas I might have had about April being a month in spring. Mr Robert Browning would not have had such nostalgic 'home thoughts from abroad' had he known an April like this. It was a cold, grey day with a strong north-easterly wind barging down from the Fens, and neither duffel coat nor wind-cheater could keep it out. We were piloted through Hermitage Lock and then left to our own resources.

As we made our way nervously along the Old West River, I had the feeling that I could already sense the spirit of those days before the Fens were drained. There was a gentle wildness about the river as we glided through reeded banks and gathering mists. The slow chug of the engine, pulsing like a heart-beat into the silence, added to the thrill of adventure. Away from the roads and familiar landmarks, the atmosphere became increasingly primeval, as if we were the first people ever to venture so far into the interior. The river smell came from the beginnings of time. Bird calls belonged to the earliest days of creation.

After two hours we decided to moor for the night and chose what we hoped would be a suitably safe stretch of bank. The sound of hammering in the mooring pins rang over the deserted landscape, betraying our presence.

One of the first things I had discovered was that you do not actually see much of the Fens from a river. High flood-banks hide the view. It is only when you stop and climb to the top of the banks that you have any idea of what the land looks like on the other side. The evening fields looked ancient and uncultivated under the mist. There was no sign of life, no hint of the generous crops to come. Our lighted boat rested on the water like a small ark which had drifted in from another age. With a feeling of apprehension and uncertainty, we locked ourselves in, prepared supper and then slept as if we really were the only survivors left on earth.

The following morning I woke early, possibly before daybreak, though in the grey light it was difficult to tell. Suddenly, out of the silence, came the sound of larks. First one, then another, then several. I was anxious to be out on the river-bank to listen more closely to their ecstatic, almost hysterical singing. There was a heavy frost on the grass, and the air was as cold as winter.

I had not walked far when out of the shadows emerged a man and his dog. Although he was civil to me, he was clearly hostile to the idea of having pleasure-boats on this stretch of water.

'They should never be allowed,' he said, pointing with his walking-stick to our small craft. 'They're much too big for a river like this. Do untold damage. There soon won't be a natural piece of bank left. It's nearly all shored up with steel or asbestos as it is. Come another few weeks and it'll be more like Brand's Hatch along here.'

Erosion is undoubtedly a serious problem and, even at this slack time of the year, I could see how the wash of some boats had bitten angrily into the banks. One had passed us on the previous evening at a speed which must have been greatly in excess of the limit.

After breakfast we moved off towards Pope's Corner and our first full day on the water. There we joined the Great Ouse and turned left for Ely. The mist lifted enough to give us a hint of sun, and there was a swish of wind through the dry reed-ronds.

Gradually I became aware of other bird calls—pheasants, peewits and ducks, and, somewhere across the fields, I could hear the bells of a parish church. Floating in what had already become a timeless zone, I had forgotten it was Sunday, and the distant sounds had a dream-like effect upon me. And then, out of the haze, emerged the shape of Ely Cathedral, becalmed like a ship on the horizon.

We arrived in Ely in time to walk round the city before making our way to the Minster Tavern for refreshments. Afterwards we continued our journey down-stream to join the River Lark. There was a wonderfully crisp, crystal-clear light which made the sky look even more expansive than ever, especially from the middle of the river, where we also had the benefit of its reflection.

The River Lark is not as attractive as its name, at least not on the surface, but I grew fond of it. It is a quiet waterway with a character of its own and penetrates deep into the Fens. I was particularly taken with Prickwillow. It had a good atmosphere and *felt* right. The people we met were warm and friendly, their village was tidy and clean, and there were the added interests of the Drainage Engine Museum and a good pottery shop run by Margot and Derek Andrews, two skilled and amiable designer-potters with several distinctive lines in their work.

Further downstream we passed another monument to

the history of Fen drainage—the steam-engine pump house, which was built in 1842 and earned for itself a reputation commemorated in verse:

> In fitness for the urgent hour,
> Unlimited, untiring power,
> Precision, promptitude, command
> The infant's will, the giant's hand.
> Steam, mighty steam ascends the throne
> And reigns lord paramount alone.

The Victorians were certainly not slow to celebrate their achievements. Steam for them was as revolutionary as nuclear power is for us today. Perhaps it is a little more difficult to get poetic about a nuclear reactor!

Once again the narrower river took on a more primitive character, and with it returned that sense of exploring the unknown which we had experienced when first setting out.

As soon as we had moored, I hurried up the bank to see what view awaited me. The scene would have amazed, if not excited, even the most unenthusiastic traveller in the Fens. Acres of rich, crumbly black peat soil for as far as the eye could see, and an earth smell as tangy as the sea.

Standing alone on the bank, I was struck by the deep, tense silence all around. It was not prolonged or unbroken. It would, perhaps, have been almost unbearable had it been so. The silence could be measured only in moments—the moments between the pheasants' cries over the dark fields; the moments between the whirr of wild ducks' wings as they flew through the returning mist, or the moments between some unexplained splash or ripple on the water. But, in those moments, the silence was electrifying enough to make me shudder.

I looked down at the boat. It appeared tiny and insignificant tucked into the elbow of the bank, but as we locked ourselves in again, we felt more secure, more confident as we turned out the lights and slept.

Because I had to be back in Ely the next morning to record a radio interview, for a programme about the Fens to be broadcast in Germany, we were forced to leave the discovery of the Little Ouse and the River Wissey for another time. Also, because the weather was getting colder by the minute, we decided that it might be wiser to make for the River Cam and flirt briefly again with civilization in Cambridge.

The Cam eventually offers a little more variety of scenery with its tree-lined banks, attractive villages and more open aspect. At least you can see something of the landscape from the boat. By the time we had passed through Upware, it was like drifting gratefully into a different season, if not a different world. As the earth responded to the warmth of the sun, the character of the journey changed.

By early evening we had moored near Shrubb's Wharf and sat down to enjoy that special kind of stillness which is found on a river. Beyond the fields and railway lines the sun slowly and perceptibly slipped towards the horizon. Its warmth was spent now and, as the air cooled, the last sounds of the day became amplified in the stillness. Calls of pheasants and ducks echoed more loudly over the fields. It was not a spectacular sunset. It faded, like an oil-lamp running out of fuel.

After a leisurely breakfast we agreed it was time to accept the challenge of Bottisham Lock and slowly eased the boat away from its mooring. It was too early to stop for lunch at the Bridge Hotel, Waterbeach, but we made a note of it for our return journey. Having done rather well at Bottisham (so we thought), we approached Baits Bite Lock with more confidence and were disappointed to find it was operated by a lock-keeper.

At Fenditton we discovered the Plough Inn and immediately decided to bring lunch forward by thirty minutes. By now appetites were growing, and at least two of us were brave enough to try a 'Big Daddy', which is a large roll of garlic bread filled with bacon, kidneys and mushrooms, with a portion of French fries to give it support.

Satisfactorily refreshed and warm again, we returned to the boat and chugged happily into the centre of Cambridge. It is surprising how, even after a few days away from noise, the sound of traffic assaults the ears. The constant roar and continual smells were offensive to the senses which had so recently experienced a pastoral way of life.

But not even the noisy roads of a city could deprive us of

The River Cam, with its tree-lined banks

the pleasure of walking round the college Backs—St John's, Trinity, King's—their paths lined with primroses and daffodils. There is an atmosphere and an elegance about these buildings which awaken a sense of pride in the soul. They are so much part of England and have nourished minds which have enriched our culture for five hundred years.

When we woke in the morning, it had turned much colder and a light rain was falling. After shopping, and an excellent lunch at the Blue Boar, we left the city to return to the countryside. The rain became increasingly heavy and persistent. By the time we had gone through Baits Bite Lock again, we were very wet and feeling weather-beaten. An early mooring was called for, and so we pulled up at Waterbeach, where, conveniently, we were able to walk up to the Bridge Hotel for a well-earned evening drink and a sit by the open log-fire.

Such was the fickleness of the weather that the following morning we were blessed again with clear skies and dazzling sunshine. Frost on the grass soon dispersed and the day looked full of promise. With lighter hearts we made our way back to Ely and then on to Brandon Creek (or the Little Ouse). As we turned from the main river into the tributary, we passed the Ship Inn at Brandon and I was reminded of those legendary days of story-telling as recalled in W. H. Barrett's *Tales from the Fens*, where men like Chafer Legge sat night after night entertaining the customers with amusing or dramatic sagas of Fenland life. It was even more extraordinary to remember that on several occasions one of those customers was none other than the great American story-teller Mark Twain, who was recuperating in the Fens after a breakdown.

Once again we moored the boat well upstream, and I climbed the bank to see what view I would be offered this time. I don't think I have ever gasped so loudly or been so amazed. Some people react like this, I imagine, on the tops of mountains or overlooking the Grand Canyon, but nothing could have given me a greater sense of wonder than the scene which greeted me that evening. If I thought the soil was black in Holme Fen, or blacker still in Burnt Fen, it was even blacker here and in such superb condition. A perfect example of good agriculture in the Fens. The land was divided by a narrow dyke which cut the scene in half. On my right were about thirty acres of winter-sown barley, emerald green and shining in the mellow light. On my left were twenty-five acres which were just being planted with potatoes. The seed potatoes had already been dressed with fertilizer and looked more like large pebbles in the lorry which fed them to the tractor and planter. Beyond these fields the black furrows converged towards Burnt Fen and, on the distant horizon, I could see Ely Cathedral. The flatness and openness were broken only by a few slender rows of poplars which were meant to serve as windbreaks, but they were no more than decorations and, in a way, out of place in that landscape.

Although it was half-past five, the men were still working, and when they returned to the lorry for a further supply of seed, I was able to talk to them. I commented on the marvellous picture the land presented and one of them said, 'That's all right today but you should be out here when the wind blows. That's a different picture then.'

I referred to the lines of trees which hemmed some of the fields and said that I couldn't imagine them being very effective in a Fen-blow.

'Not now they ain't cus they've bin too thinned out. I've seen eighty acres of trees disappear from this fen in the last few years.'

'Are you for trees, or against them?'

''For, I think. But you've got to do it properly. There used to be three rows of poplars round this field once.'

'How many acres are there on this farm?'

'Five hundred.'

'It's worth a bit, then?'

'When it were sold three year ago, that went for just over a million pounds. Ten years ago that sold for £126,000.'

'That really is inflation.'

'You could say that.'

'You need to be wealthy to own land out here.'

'Not many farmers actually own their farms in the Fens these days; they can't afford to. Most of the land around here is owned by pension funds or insurance companies in other parts of the country.'

'What sort of tonnage will you be hoping for from this field?'

'Twenty tons an acre, I should think. We'll be disappointed if it's less.'

''You're putting in a long day, aren't you?'

'We'll be packing up at six.'

'And what time do you start in the morning?'

'Five-thirty.'

I left the men to finish their day's work and returned to the boat. Later that evening my wife and I went for a walk along the edge of the fields, and I knew at that moment I was getting close to whatever it was I had gone to find.

For me the true spirit of the Fens is to be found on a calm spring evening, at the end of a working day, in the silence of the fields and all they contain—the past, the present and what is to be; the sown and the unsown; the garnered and the forgotten, and in the ghosts and remembrances of those men whose bones have ached and rejoiced at redeeming this rich earth from an ancient wilderness.

True enough, the sound of tractors woke me before six o'clock, and I went up again to take another look at that remarkable sight.

'I just can't get over the blackness of it,' I said to one of the men.

'Black? That's not black, that's brown. If you want to see black fens, you should go over to Feltwell. Now that *is* black.'

It was difficult to drag myself away from such a scene but it was time to begin the last stage of our holiday. No ocean or mountain range could have filled me with such awe. The land had a hidden power which was magnetic, even mesmeric, and I felt the blood pumping through my veins as if it recognized the history of its origins.

The voyage into the interior had taken me back to an age of which I have no conscious recollection, but which I knew held part of my being. To leave it was like being evicted from one's home, and the journey back to Earith was longer than can be measured by any river, or any man. It becomes part of one's life, a heart-beat pulsing quietly through the veins forever.

8 'One Spot Beloved Over All . . .'

Some friends from Australia once said to me that the one aspect of England which they always enjoyed was the unpredictability of the weather. 'You can never be sure that two days are going to be alike, whatever the season. Here we are in April and it's cold enough for snow. And tomorrow it will no doubt be blazing like a day in July. Back home we know where we are with our seasons, and it gets a bit monotonous. Over here you can have a whole year's weather in one week, which is great.'

I was pleased that they could see it that way, and I realized again how necessary it is, from time to time, to see this land through the eyes of the visitor so as not to take its virtues too much for granted.

I remember, too, how thrilled I was two springs ago when my parents-in-law came over from Canada to explore my native landscape for the first time. When I took them out for their baptismal drive, I knew luck was with me. The Fens put on a most beguiling appearance for them, and even I could not refrain from an additional gasp of admiration.

The weather helped, of course, and although it has been said before that if you can't love the Fens on a wet day, you can't love them at all, it does make a difference if you can give strangers their first look at them on a lovely spring morning when the light and the space and the sky can actually be seen. That important day could not have been more co-operative. It had everything I could have hoped for, and more. Perhaps I should not sound so surprised. I ought to know by now that this landscape can catch you unawares on almost any occasion. It is unpredictable and should never be taken for granted. Just when you think you know it intimately, it will suddenly produce an aspect or a mood never experienced before and the amazement starts all over again.

Between the Easter and Whitsun of that spring we had a world slowly turning golden with the generous acreage of oil-seed rape being grown that year. It made the earth dazzle. Whichever way the eye turned, there was an expanse of yellow which intensified the sharp, crystal light of the sky. The air, too, was golden and heady with the smell of the crops, giving the day a touch of dreamy unreality.

We drove out through Abbots Ripton, Wennington, Raveley and Wistow. All round us was that tremendous display of men's labours and expertise in cultivating this land reminding us yet again that we live in a predominantly man-made landscape reclaimed from wilderness and marsh, a land which has been farmed for generations by the same families of both land-owners and farm-workers, and I am aware of the fact that without them there would be no Fen country, as we know it now.

I say 'as we know it now' because we must remember that the term 'Fen country' is itself a misnomer in these days of efficient drainage. After all, what is a 'Fen'? One dictionary says: 'A fen is a low, marshy area of land often under water; a morass or bog.' Such a definition was true, on a large scale, two hundred years ago, but not now. The only real surviving Fens are the small nature reserves such as Wicken and Woodwalton, but even with these we are getting no more than a civilized glimpse of our wilder past. Even so, I cannot imagine this landscape being called anything else, and perhaps it is indicative of our stubbornness and defiance that we have retained the former geographical name for it.

From the rise between Wood Walton village and Abbots Ripton there is usually a fine panorama of the nearby Fens which man has created out of that original morass, but, on that particular day, I could not conceal my deep, satisfying pride as I shared the view with those seeing it for the first time. As well as the oil-seed rape there were acres of wheat, barley and potatoes all growing towards fruition in that rich, black soil which still kept hidden much of its history.

The present has meaning only when seen against the failures or successes of the past, and an appreciation of any landscape is greatly enriched by an awareness of what has gone before. Not only has the Fen country been fought over by Man and Nature for thousands of years but there have been conflicts between the Church and the State, between landowner and landowner. Each newly turned furrow could, I am sure, tell its own story, and, in a way, it does.

We continued our tour and, at the appropriate hour, called at a suitable hostelry for a pub lunch. Half-way through the first pint a yellow dog walked into the bar. I blinked, looked at my father-in-law and realized that he too was staring at the same apparition.

'Good lord,' he said, 'this English beer is stronger than I thought.'

I nodded. Then the dog shook himself, and a cloud of yellow dust filled the air. He had been hunting in the rape fields and, whatever colour he should have been, was now mustard-yellow until he'd had a bath.

As if to confirm my statement about the unpredictability of the Fens, something else happened two hours later for which I was selfishly and temporarily grateful and which, I assure you, had nothing to do with the beer. We had a 'Fen-blow'. I say 'selfishly' because I am very aware of how heart-breaking and disastrous a Fen-blow can be to farmers whose fields are being savaged by the gale-force winds. There can be no beauty or excitement in seeing your newly sown seedlings and fertilizer being blown away and scattered on someone else's land a mile off. But this was a local phenomenon which my father-in-law had not experienced before, and I was, for that moment, pleased that the drama had been produced so conveniently. There, towards the end of a perfect day which had begun with cloudless skies, was a fearsome black dust-storm, billowing over Holme Fen and Yaxley. That part of the sky darkened while all around stayed bright. It was a terrifying, almost apocalyptic moment as we sat in silence on a deserted road, watching the earth rise before us.

To explain the origins of a Fen-blow, I took my passenger round to the shores of the extinct Whittlesea Mere and Holme Woods to see the now well-known posts which have

Holme Woods—'an enchanting and haunting place'

recorded the shrinkage of the drained Fens for more than 130 years. It is an enchanting and haunting area which I shall be writing more about in a later chapter, so I will not indulge myself in superfluous descriptions of it here. It is enough to say that after such a vivid geography lesson no one can say that this landscape is dull or uninteresting. Its history, evolution, traditions and vagaries can inspire the most reluctant imagination to see a world beneath the skin which is puzzling if not compellingly magnetic.

When writing of his native county of Sussex in 1902, Rudyard Kipling said

> God gave all men all earth to love,
>   But, since our hearts are small,
> Ordains for each one spot shall prove
>   Belov'ed over all. . . .

I would never wish to argue with that. Nor, I must admit, would I always wish to have this one spot shared by others. There are times (more often than less) when a man needs his landscape all to himself. There are the secret places I would not show to anyone, or only to a very few, and even then on only the rarest occasion.

Just as the ornithologist would not reveal to the world the nesting-place of a threatened bird, so too would I not betray those small corners which I need as my sanctuary. A tuft of grass can have an identity. A dykeside of reeds can be different from all others. There are fields where the lark sings sweeter, where the light catches a blade of wheat more vividly than any other, a furrow which throbs more vibrantly with history than all the volumes ever written. There are those places, too, which have a special silence, a more positive link with the past, a more sustaining influence over the present. All fields are different. All rivers and dykes have their own character. All roads lead to somewhere which has its own purpose for being.

And so, for me, there are places which are 'beloved over all', places which have allowed me to feel a deeper sense of contentment and belonging than I have felt anywhere else. Is it because there are some small areas on this planet where time ceases to exist, where one insignificant life can be encompassed by the whole universe?

I know that I can only share with others my love of this land if I preserve these private places. I see a star fall out of the sky, burn out in the twinkling of an eye. I see a bird flit from the twig of a tree and disappear. I see a shadow pass over the water and the river remain still. And, in every infinitesimal moment, I feel the great heave and sigh of eternity.

There are sounds as well as sights. Whispers of the world which disturb the silence, echoes which nudge the sleeping earth for a second and then become still. A fish belches discreetly in the bed of a river. A hidden snail-shell crunches beneath a clumsy foot, then the deep breath of guilt. And, somewhere in the laboratory of the soil, a seed cracks into life and a harvest is born.

These are the moments when I have to say 'I am', that this world exists only because of me; and I, only because of it. The day you betray such secret places, the world ends and there is no sharing for anyone. A veil is drawn over the horizon. The door to the temple is closed.

9 A Fenland Abbey or Two

Most of us, I believe, have a favourite place, however modest, which stays in the affections long after more impressive places have been forgotten. It might be a house, a town, a historic building or a particular landscape which has this appeal, because of either a pleasant association or a treasured memory. Sometimes we may not even know why a place has such a demand on our attentions; all we do know is that it has become part of us and we would feel lost without it. Again and again, we return to the same small seaside resort or holiday farmhouse, to the same picnic spot or village tea-shop because it is where we shall always feel at home and at peace with ourselves.

A place for which I have had a special affection now for nearly forty years is Crowland Abbey. I know I have written about it before and ought not to extend my feelings for it here, but I have been drawn back to it time and time again in all weathers and seasons of the year, and each time it is different. I see or experience something not seen or felt before. Ever since I discovered it many years ago while exploring the Fens on an old, second-hand bike which was given to me during the war years, I have responded to it as iron-filings to a magnet.

It was a claw-sharp day then, with an unfriendly wind blowing in from the North Sea, and I knew nothing of the abbey's history or of its significance in the dramatic story of the Fens. I just stood and was overwhelmed by the presence of the past, by the serenity and peace that existed within those silent stones. From that day the building became not only a magnet but a guiding-star, and its story became a source of both comfort and inspiration. Even from a distance of ten miles or more, it stands out like a beacon, saying to the traveller, 'Take care. All's well! You are nearly home.'

My feelings about Crowland Abbey were re-affirmed a few days ago when I was on my way to Spalding. One of the great benefits of having that bypass now is that an aspect of the abbey has been momentarily revealed to those travellers who might not otherwise go into the town itself to see the building at close quarters.[1] I could not pass, however, and impulsively turned off the main road and drove slowly towards the broken columns and the dog-tooth arch which never fails to excite my eyes. My detour was rewarded even more than I expected because the scaffolding which had been erected for the cleaning of the west front had been taken down, and the stone-work shone with an apricot glow in the morning sun. The figures of saints and kings took on the freshness of stone newly sculptured, and the mind was immediately transported back to a time when the whole building would have looked as sparkling and unmarred by weather or wars.

There are those, I know, who do not like to see old buildings given this kind of face-lift, who feel that the grime of ages is all part of the attraction. The initial impact at seeing a piece of antiquity scrubbed clean might be disturbing for a while, but any restoration which is going to preserve the life of a building cannot be all that wrong. A few winter fogs and rain will soon soften the hard lines brought about by such cosmetic surgery, and it does make one look at the place more carefully.

To understand the quiet power of Crowland Abbey, the imagination has to travel back even further than the present building. It has to go back to a time before the first Barnack ragstone was laid or the shape which we now take for granted was even designed. It has to go back to St Bartholomew's Day in AD 699, when a young Mercian nobleman called Guthlac chose the then inhospitable island of Crulands in the Fens as the place where he wanted to establish his religious hermitage. After many trials and tribulations he achieved all, and more, of what he had planned. He had tamed the hostile natives, healed the sick,

[1] Since this chapter was written a new housing-estate has made that aspect even more momentary.

Crowland Abbey—'a place of special affection'

founded a house of prayer, cared for wild animals who learned to eat from his hand, and prophesied that one day Prince Ethelbald would become King of Mercia. On hearing this, the prince vowed that if ever he sat upon the throne he would build a great monastery as an act of gratitude to the gentle monk of Crowland.

Sadly, Guthlac did not live to see his prophecy fulfilled. He died at the age of forty, on 11 April 714. But Ethelbald kept his promise and, on St Bartholomew's Day in 716, laid the foundation stones of the first abbey. That building, however, was not to last long. Built mainly of wood, it was to become a victim of fire and suffer total destruction by the Vikings. But the abbey was rebuilt, an even grander and more substantial place than before, only to be burnt down again in 1091, when its precious library of over seven hundred illuminated manuscripts was tragically lost in flames. It seemed that Crowland was not to be. Yet the phoenix rose from the ashes again and, despite further destruction by fire and earthquake, it survived. The spirit of Guthlac could not be destroyed. We can now walk through the ruined nave to recapture some of its history or attend that part of it used as the parish church to continue the worship commenced by the eccentric hermit who became a saint.

When you go, stand for a moment on the grass of the nave and look towards that delicate Norman arch poised like a stone rainbow in the sky. You will feel the spirit of the Fens as well there as it can be felt anywhere. You will stand where kings and traitors have stood, where martyrs and murderers have come face to face, where once the shadow of Hereward the Wake fell across the path on which you walk. Look beyond the broken columns and see the Fens stretching away towards a far horizon. You will not be unmoved. In the stillness you might almost feel some ghostly figure at your back—as Richard Mardick did in L. P. Hartley's novel *The Brickfield*. You might even believe that in the distance you can see the misty outline of a Viking longboat inching its way upstream. With the cawing of the rooks will be mingled the shouts and screams of those who fought and died there—Abbot Theodore, who was murdered at the altar steps while praying for his attackers, or the frightened cries of the boy-monk Turgar crouched in the shadows.

Despite its turbulent history, it is for me a place of unparalleled serenity, a place to heal the spirit made weary sometimes by the clamours of today. It is a place where you can be made to feel at one with the past and, in doing so, find sustenance for the present.

You can see how dangerous it is to break a journey just to look at some old ruins. I can't remember now whether I ever got to Spalding that day or not. What I do know is that I would not have missed the experience for all the money in the world. It was a good day, a memorable day, a day enhanced by the warmth of spring, the eager song of the skylarks and the shimmering green light over the fields. A day that St Guthlac would have enjoyed as he waited for the first swallows to arrive at his cell window. Legend has it that they would perch on his shoulder and wait for instruction as to where they could build their nests. The swallows and martins still come but now please themselves—or perhaps they have inherited their nesting-sites from all that long ago and know where to build.

Another abbey which I think would have had the same hypnotic power had it survived would have been Sawtry. A much newer abbey by comparison—it was not built until 1146—it nevertheless earned a reputation as a refuge and a sanctuary for all those who found their own troubled times difficult to withstand. It was a generous, charitable abbey, as we are reminded from the old Fenland rhyme:

Ramsey the rich of gold and fee
Thorney the flower of many fair tree
Croyland the courteous of meat and drink
Spalding the gluttons as all men do think
Peterborough the proud as all men do say
Sawtry, by the way, that old abbey
Gave more alms in one day than all they.

Like Crowland, Thorney, Peterborough and many more Fenland abbeys, Sawtry was built of Barnack stone brought down by the barges on the Nene and across Whittlesea Mere. It owned a great area of land, including Monks Wood, and so could afford to be charitable, as indeed most abbeys could. The Cistercian monks who built that abbey had to get permission from Pope Alexander III to cross land which belonged to the Benedictine monastery at Ramsey. There was much rivalry between the abbeys then, and Christian love must have been in short supply on many occasions as the abbots fought long legal battles for possession of land and rents. The disputes were not always settled in the courts either. More than a few skirmishes took place between the religious communities over their boundaries and rights of way.

It was at Sawtry Abbey that Queen Catherine of Aragon's body rested on its way to Peterborough for burial. One is constantly reminded of how the historical events of hundreds of years cast a web of associations over all the abbeys in the Fens. Some, like Peterborough and Ely, are still with us in all their magnificence. Others, like Crowland and Ramsey, can only tease us now with their shattered remains, leaving the rest to our imaginations. Some, like Sawtry, challenge our imaginations even more, and, as we look across the fertile farmlands between Sawtry Fen and Wood Walton, it may be a little harder to hear the echoes of plainsong or chant, or to hear the tolling of a bell calling those hooded ghosts to prayer. But, on a day when the light is right, when there is a calmness in the air, it is possible to believe that just over there, in the middle of a field, stands a building reflecting the evening sun.

Sometimes a plough turns up a piece of stone that was once part of an abbey, and then the stone speaks with an eloquence it may not have had even in its pristine days. The land around us is full of clues. Beneath the hidden paths are ways we can still follow. And the atmosphere grows heady again with the scent of history.

I remember a few years ago visiting a farm house where the bowl of a font was being used as a feeding-trough. When I asked the farmer where it came from, he said, 'Oh, that's been there as long as I can remember. I think my old dad found it when he was clearing out some rubble from the bottom field.' At least the stone from Thorney Abbey—that 'flower of many fair tree'—was put to better use when four-fifths of it went to help build the colleges of Cambridge University.

But it is to Crowland I return, not because I hear its warning-bell telling of impending floods (or because its peal of bells was among the first to be broadcast in England) but because on a spring day it rises again from a land which has, temporarily been saved from the water and stands now as a symbol of survival, stability and hope. When the days grow warmer, will the bees be back, I wonder, busily buzzing their way in and out of the stone walls as I have often watched them do before? There are times when you can hear the side of the church hum with the activity of these secret chambers. Did St Guthlac once give them permission, too, to build their hives on his holy island? Perhaps.

10 Shadow of Genius

Several years ago a Yorkshireman wrote to me after reading one of my books to tell me of his interest in my home town of Whittlesey, and from that simple beginning has developed a remarkable story.

Mr Bertram Winterton is now in his eightieth year and has, for the past forty-two years, lived in Girton. He is also a very versatile artist and still captures the spirit of the Fens in both water-colours and oils.

As he explained in his first letter to me, 'my father was a Whittlesey man by birth, so I love both the Yorkshire Dales and the Fens.'

His grandmother and aunt lived opposite the Falcon Hotel, and in 1923 he cycled all the way from York to visit them. 'I still remember', he wrote, 'lying in bed listening to the chimes and hymn-tunes of the church of St Mary.'

What he did not know then was that, forty-two years later, he would be designing a new inn-sign for that hotel, as he did for many other hostelries in the Fens; most, alas, now painted over by other hands.

But it was not about himself that he wished to write. He wanted to tell me of another young man in Whittlesey who had shown great promise as a poet before dying in 1827 at the age of twenty.

I must admit that I had never heard of James Spencer (who was a great-great-uncle to Mr Winterton) and was excited to learn that he was obviously a person of considerable talent, who had been published in the *Apollo Magazine*. So what else was there to discover?

Fortunately Mr Winterton had inherited a large quantity of manuscripts which he had placed for safe-keeping in the records Office, at Shire Hall, Cambridge. Next week, I promised myself, I must go over to look through them. But the weeks, and the years, passed and, with more pressing research to do on John Clare, I'm afraid that James Spencer was pushed into the background.

It was Pete Morgan's story about the Boat Inn being haunted by the ghost of someone who fell off Briggate Bridge that aroused my interest again. From Mr Winterton's second letter I learned that James Spencer's father (also James) had 'met with a most untimely end in January 1808. At the break-up of the ice he fell over Briggate Bridge and was drowned.'

I could not put off my visit to Shire Hall any longer and, on a bright spring day, drove over the Fens to Cambridge. In the warmth and quietness of the Records Office I sat and looked at the piles of documents and manuscripts before me. All this, I thought, from a young man who was not twenty-one?

Most of the manuscripts were in home-made notebooks, made out of notices of sale and other sale bills issued from the solicitor's office where Spencer worked. The hand writing was copper-plate but miniscule, the subjects so varied it was difficult to believe that so many ideas had come from one so young and poorly educated.

There were essays on Ancient Greece, Egyptology, history, religion and the art of novel-writing, detailed studies of the Old Testament, and many poems. There was also a draft of a 'legal address to the Public for subscribers to a proposed publication of poems'. This was written in 1822 on the back of a 'Notice of Sale of Property in Scalgate'. It was a short autobiography and just what I was looking for:

> I was born on the 4th day of June in the year 1807 of respectable parents, whose circumstances never rose above mediocrity; my father was a hairdresser and clerk of the parish. When I was 8 months old a lamentable accident made me an orphan, and left me with a brother and a sister of infantile years, to the care of a widowed mother. Heaven enabled her to provide for us all in a comfortable manner and I reached my 10th year with all the happiness imaginable. I had always been a keen lover of letters and fortunately at this period a friend of my father's stepped forward to assist in my education. I was placed at the best

> school in the Parish and there I acquired what little knowledge I possess of the classics, and imbibed a thirst for learning and literary honours, my Master himself teaching me Latin without the extra premium. I was his favourite scholar and he my beloved teacher. . . . At his school I stayed 3 years; when my friend withdrew his assistance, and left me with my education to begin the world with. My first situation was with a relation, whose accounts I kept and subsequently I became Clerk to a Conveyor, who I left in July 1822. . . . Since then I have been in my present capacity which is that of a clerk (unarticled) to Mr Bellars, an Attorney of this place, who allows me a very trifling salary, but I am indebted (to him) for the midnight lamp and the hours which succeed a sedentary day. To the same source I owe my library which is purchased with the scanty earnings of industrious moments stolen from repose; but this would be of little utility [?] had not village fame procured me admittance to some libraries around.

I could not help but compare that account of Spencer's beginnings with the early strivings of John Clare. But what of the poetry which was being written by this young man with some 'village fame' in Whittlesey? Like Clare, he longed for a better education and for a greater skill with words. In some lines to Lord Byron (one of his idols) he wrote:

> I would I had that flame poetic which
> Burn'd in thy breast & lighted on thy page;
> That spirit of invention none can teach
> And none can give—not Art's, but Nature's rage
> Romantic. . . .

Again like Clare, Spencer drew on local scenes and village life for his inspiration:

> I reach'd a village one fine afternoon
> Blest with May's sunshine at the mellow hour
> When village clocks strike four—a sound that soon
> In ev'ry street display'd its wondrous pow'r. . . .

And the power of the clocks striking four was to stop everyone working at whatever daily tasks each villager performed, bringing them home to fireside and family, where, in the evenings, they would re-tell old favourite stories.

Hark! how the oak-riving tempest roars without
And, forcing entrance at my chimney-tops
Howls to the subject blaze: the embers fanned
Upon the broad, rais'd hearth with many a spark
And smoky wreath. . . .

That verse especially reminded me of the Helpston poet, writing of a similar scene:

The winter wind with strange & fearful gust
Stirs the dark wood & in the lengthy night
Howls in the chimney top while fear's mistrust
Listens the noise by the small glimmering light
Of Cottage hearth where warm a circle sits
Of happy dwellers telling morts of tales. . . .

Spencer did not achieve Clare's mastery of mood or language, nor is there any evidence from his lists of reading that he had ever heard of Clare, whose fame was already declining by the time Spencer died. But there is proof, I think, in the work which this twenty-year-old poet left behind, that there was the shadow of genius, and, if he could have lived and enjoyed the opportunities which had come to Clare, who knows what greatness he might also have achieved?

I left the Records Office feeling that I had been in the presence of a remarkable young man, a boy who had walked the streets of my home town and listened to the church clock chiming away the hours, just as I had done when I went to school there.

Since my visit to Cambridge I have also met Mr Winterton, and it was like meeting someone I had known for a very long time. In the studio which he built for himself at the bottom of the garden I was able to look through a collection of paintings which spanned a lifetime. Here, too,

The Buttercross at Whittlesey where James Spencer 'enjoyed some village fame'

was evidence of a talent that had been quietly recording those moments 'it would otherwise impoverish us to forget.' Some of his Fen landscapes particularly appealed to me.

As I turned to leave, Mr Winterton pointed to a small silhouette on the wall. 'There he is. That's James Spencer!'

I looked at the handsome profile. What a different story it might have been if that young man had walked with Keats, or Shelley, or John Clare!

James Spencer was buried in St Mary's churchyard, and it was inevitable that I should revisit Whittlesey again to imagine it as he might have known it between 1807 and 1827. The bells of St Mary's have had their musical chimes restored, and the ancient Buttercross is still there. So, too, are many of the buildings he would have passed on his way to work. But it is a far different town from the one he would have known. The traffic alone would have been a vision of hell in his day, and modern development has not added to whatever charm the town once possessed.

It is, however, worth remembering that in Spencer's time the population of Whittlesey was as large as Peterborough's, and there was probably more social life than there is today—for some. A few years before Spencer was born, the town had become a garrison for both the Durham and Westminster Militia, with several companies stationed there each year. The young ladies found themselves in great demand at the dinners and garden-parties organized by the officers. Afternoon tea-drinking became so fashionable it was often considered decadent by those who were not privileged to enjoy it.

The presence of the military no doubt went some way towards inspiring one young Whittlesey man to enlist in the 95th Rifle Brigade in 1805. His name was Henry Smith, later to become famous as Sir Harry Smith who, in 1846, distinguished himself as the hero of Aliwal under Clive of India. Two years later Sir Harry was made Governor of the Cape of Good Hope, where he, and Lady Smith, were much loved by the people. He is remembered in his home town mainly by the Sir Harry Smith Community College and a pub called 'The Hero of Aliwal'. The house where he was born still stands in St Mary's Street, and there are commemorative plaques in the church. But his is another story. . . .

In 1832, five years after James Spencer's death, a severe epidemic of cholera broke out in the area, and by the end of May several Whittlesey people had died from it and a number of businesses were closed down. The town also appears to have had its share of fires. Certainly, as a child, I can remember being taken to see two or three serious fires where rows of houses were burnt to the ground. This was nothing new to the town, for it had frequently been devastated during the previous eight hundred years. In April 1244 it was virtually destroyed completely. Most of the houses were razed to their foundations, including the two churches, and forty-two people were burnt to death. The town was rebuilt, only to be reduced again to ashes thirty years later. From local newspaper reports during the nineteenth century it is clear that fires continued to be a scourge of the town. In 1809 fire 'consumed many houses' and left people homeless. On 18 June 1870 one local paper reported: 'An alarming and destructive fire occurred at Whittlesey. Eleven cottages were burned to the ground, and an entire range of premises 150 yards deep and 100 yards long, were a burning mass. It was estimated that at least three or four acres of buildings were reduced to ruins. The flames were eventually extinguished by a heavy thunderstorm.'

Had the young James Spencer lived, he would, I'm sure, have written a fine history of Whittlesey, for he had an inquiring mind, loved research and also had a fine gift for words. Had Time been kinder to him, he too would have brought honour to the town and would be less forgotten than he is today, for, as the *Lincoln, Rutland and Stamford Mercury* said in announcing his death: 'He was a young man of great natural genius and ability.'

11 Times Remembered at a Five-barred Gate

I met Madge one Monday morning as she walked along the edge of a ploughed field, near Postland. She wore a faded black beret which had shrunk almost to a skull-cap, a belted raincoat which had absorbed the weathers of at least forty years, and a pair of Wellingtons which had stomped over as many furrows as anyone could plough in a lifetime. At her heels ambled a black Labrador, who wore an expression of resignation rather than enthusiasm.

I watched Madge as she approached, and her eyes never looked up. I even thought she might pass me by without noticing that I was there. Her head was bent forward and she stared at the ground with a look which found it easier to peer intensely at nothing rather than at something in particular.

I did not know her name then, for I had never seen her before. I had simply stopped to look over a five-barred gate at a newly ploughed field, when along came this figure like a ghost out of the mist, if not the past.

'Morning!' I said tentatively.

She stopped and looked at me. 'You don't come from round here, do you?'

'No, I live in Peterborough.'

'Peterborough? I bet that's changed since I last saw it.'

'When was that?'

'Twenty-five years ago, I should think.'

I assured her that the city had changed very much and expressed some surprise that she had not more frequently visited a place that was only nine miles away.

'I don't go out much. Don't see much point in it myself. You only meet people, and noise, and traffic. I prefer my own company.'

'You live round here?'

Times remembered at a five-barred gate

'Over there,' she said with a jerk of the head.

'Do you like the Fens?'

''They're all right I suppose. Wouldn't want to live anywhere else.'

'Do you live alone?'

'I do now. My husband was killed on the farm thirty years ago, and my son left home after we'd had a tiff. Haven't seen him for nigh on twelve year.'

'What's your dog's name?'

'You ask a lot of bloody questions, don't you? Who are you?'

I apologized and avoided an explanation by asking another question.

'Did you work on the land?'

'Of course. Done everything but beet-chopping. Once saw a gel chop three fingers off doing that job. That's not for me, I said.'

'How old were you when you started work?'

'Eleven, maybe twelve. No more.'

That answer stopped my questioning for a moment, and I could not help thinking what a coincidence it was that I had just been reading some extracts from the memoirs of a Mrs

Burrows, who had lived as a child in Crowland during 1850–60. Recalling those years she wrote:

> On the day that I was eight years of age, I left school and began to work fourteen hours a day in the fields, with from forty to fifty other children, of whom, even at that early age, I was the eldest. We were followed all day long by an old man carrying a long whip, which he did not forget to use. A great many of the children were only five years of age. . . . We always left the town, summer and winter, the moment the old abbey clock struck six. We had to walk a very long way to our work, very often five miles each way. The large farms all lay a good distance from the town and it was on those farms that we worked. In the winter, by the time we reached our work, it was light enough to begin, and of course we worked until it was dark and then had our long walk home. . . . In the summer we did not leave the fields in the evening until the clock had struck six. In all the four years I worked in the fields I never worked one hour under cover of a barn, and only once did we have a meal in a house. And I shall never forget that one meal or the woman who gave us it. It was a most terrible day. The cold east wind (no wind ever blew colder), the sleet and snow, seemed almost to cut us to pieces. . . . Dinner-time came, and we were preparing to sit down under a hedge and eat our cold dinner, and drink our cold tea, when we saw the shepherd's wife coming towards us, and she said to the ganger, 'Bring these children into my house and let them eat their dinner there.' We went into that very small two-roomed cottage, and when we got into the largest room there was not standing room for us all . . . so she put her few chairs and table out into the garden, and then we all sat down in a ring upon the floor. She then placed in our midst a very large saucepan of hot boiled potatoes and bade us help ourselves. . . . She was one of the plainest women I ever knew; in fact she was what the world would call ugly, and yet I can't think of her even now without thinking of that verse in one of our hymns where it says:
>
> > 'No, Earth has angels though their forms are moulded
> > But of such clay as fashions all below. . . .'

I looked at Madge. I had no idea whether she was one of

earth's angels or not, but she was plain and made of 'such clay'. She may not have known times quite as hard as Mrs Burrows', but hardship was deeply ingrained in her wrinkled face, and hopelessness, if not bitterness, dwelt in her hollow eyes.

'What were conditions like when you started work?'

She still looked at the ground and shook her head. 'Terrible! They'd never get away with it today. Nobody would stand for what we had to put up with. It's gone too far the other way now.'

'How many hours a day did you work?'

'Never less than ten. We always started at six and were allowed twenty minutes for our dockey. In winter we finished at four, in summer we worked till it got dark, six days a week, and then chapel on Sundays, three times a day.'

'Did you mind going to chapel?'

'We had no choice. It was all right I suppose. We used to sing and keep warm, but I'm sure now that we listened to a lot of claptrap.'

'You don't go now?'

'No. Most of the chapels round here are closed down now. Once upon a time there was hardly a street without a chapel, and most of 'em were well attended. We used to have Sunday School outings to Hunstanton or Mablethorpe, and Anniversaries. Now they're all garages, or pulled down. Times have changed since then.'

Certainly during the nineteenth century the towns and villages of the Fens had almost as many chapels as you would have found in South Wales. The Methodist movement, together with the Baptists and Congregationalists, offered an attractive alternative, politically as well as spiritually, to the Church of England. The social differences were underlined and made clear even in religion. I remember one morning, at our local C of E school, the headmaster saying, 'Hands up all those who go to church.'

Surprised that so many hands hovered nervously in the air, he quickly said, 'And chapel doesn't count.'

Most of our hands dropped quickly to our sides and we felt not only a sense of relief but also of criticism, chastisement, even betrayal. We were not God's elect, it seemed, if we did not worship in the proper place; nor would we have been happy there. Our parents followed Wesley and William Booth and loved a fiery sermon with boisterous hymns. My father had little time for a preacher who needed notes. He liked a sermon 'to come straight from the heart', and the more outspoken it was the better. Prayers read from a book were even more frowned upon.

But, as Madge said, even the faith of the zealous eventually wore thin, and when the loyal few died, there were few younger people to take their place. There were other religions now, and the names of Ebenezer, Bethesda, Primitive and Zion no longer admonish us from their sacred walls. If the buildings remain at all, the name-stones stare down sadly at us like unused theatre masks. The actors are missing, the lines forgotten, the plot of the drama is lost.

It was whilst we were talking about chapels that a man rode by on his bike and called out, 'Morning, Madge. All right?'

At least I knew her name, if not her dog's, and somehow the spell was broken. I could ask no more questions. It was time to leave Madge in her world and go in search of my own. For a few lost moments I had no idea where to go, or where to begin. I had forgotten why I was there or what I had planned to do with the day, other than drift.

I drove slowly through Holbeach Drove, Gedney Hill, up to Sutton St Edmund, and down to Parson Drove. But nothing happened. The landscape stared back at me as if I had no right to be there. Not even the thought that Samuel Pepys had been there and found it a 'heathen place' raised my spirit. In any case I did not find Parson Drove any more heathen than anywhere else.

On such occasions, when not even the sky or the land will inspire, there is nothing to do but return home and make of the day what you can. Like an angler who knows that the fish will not bite however long he sits there, so the writer also knows there are days when thoughts lie stubbornly on the muddy river-bed of the mind and no bait will make them move.

I felt grateful that I had met Madge who had brought to the surface memories I had buried long ago. Wasn't that enough for one day?

12 Reclaiming Lost Worlds

There is something very strange and unsettling about actually stepping back into the past rather than just recollecting it from a distance.

I was made aware of this when I was involved in the making of the television programme I mentioned earlier. It was a lovely late September day, and the sun felt warmer than it had been all summer. We started filming in Whittlesey at nine in the morning, and the light had a sharpness which gave even the most ordinary things a special quality. When we moved from the ancient Butter-cross to the ancient school which I had attended, I was intrigued by the ease with which we can claim back the years. Was it so long ago that I last walked through those gates? It felt like only yesterday, and the disused playground echoed again with the familiar names and voices.

From the moment I stepped into that playground, I was a boy again, making my way up the steps to the porch. As I stepped inside, I half-expected to see the classrooms and the desks exactly as I left them. I expected also to see the other boys sitting there and to hear the teachers' voices shouting at us—'Brown, Coulson, Henson, Oliver, Smith, Storey. . . .' But the school is now used as a Roman Catholic church and, where there used to be three class-rooms, there was now just one room which formed the main part of the church, and an altar had taken the place of the antiquated tortoise-stove which used to belch out its smelly heat to keep us warm. All had changed and yet all was still the same. The only feature which really took me by surprise was the roof, which had not changed but which I had forgotten. Those heavy oak beams must have always been there, but I had never noticed them or, if I had, their beauty had not impressed me.

Beyond the vestry door was the room where I think I fell in love with English literature, where, on Friday after noons, Miss Speechley read to us from the 'Classics' and produced in me a longing to use words which seemed to belong to a different language from the one I was accustomed to hearing.

From the school the T.V. crew moved out into the Fens and, apart from an occasional farm vehicle, we were not troubled too much by noise. As I stood there, waiting for the camera-man and producer to set up their first shots, I looked across the land and felt again that unmistakable affection for it, an affection that has deepened with understanding. I was there to say something of that affection, to explain what it was about the Fens that inspired me so much. It was just the feeling I needed at that moment. There is an excitement in sharing with others the beauty of a landscape which they are probably seeing for the first time. It heightens one's own awareness and sharpens the appreciation so that all the old loyalties are renewed.

The Roman Catholic Church at Whittlesey which was our school

Towards the end of the day, after filming at Chapel Bridge, Glassmoor Bank, Ramsey St Mary's and Upwood School, we arrived at Holme Fen and the site of Whittlesea Mere. The camera-man, not a native of these parts and not, I think, an ardent lover of the Fens, at that moment suddenly became totally absorbed in what the early evening light was doing to an otherwise 'dull' landscape. The low rays of the setting sun were gilding the fields with a golden lustre which even I found irresistible. The light caught the spears of corn-stubble so that each stalk shone as if it had just been brassoed. Shafts of sunlight stretched along the dykes, illuminating the slender reeds until they, too, looked heraldic—a forgotten army in miniature on the march, its banners flowing with victory. The waters in the peaty dykes were as polished steel, and the black fields held that first sheen of autumn.

The camera-man had long finished taking the shots which the producer wanted but was now engrossed in getting the pictures *he* wanted. He clambered down into the dykes and focused his camera along the narrow waterways, trying to catch the shimmering light in the reeds before it faded. He let his camera-eye rove over the low fields towards the nearby woods behind on which the sun was now setting. Even then it was as much as the rest of the film-crew could do to persuade him to 'Roll it up, Mac, and let's get home.' Reluctantly he made his way back to Norwich. Now that part of the Fens for me has been enriched by his appreciation of them then.

Whittlesea Mere is a strange, haunting and enchanting piece of Fen country. It evokes a mystery and a romance which are more than justified when you look into its history. The first accounts we have of it go back to AD 664, when King Wulphere of Mercia gave it to the then new monastery at Medeshamstede (now Peterborough). King Canute once sailed on the Mere and was caught in one of the freak storms for which this inland water was notorious. The storms were so often violent and unpredictable that they became known as 'water-quakes', and many boats became their victims. By the middle of the seventeenth century the Mere was one of the most popular places in the country for lavish regattas and water-picnics. In 1676 a party was given in honour of the Bishop of Peterborough by Mr William Pierrepont of Orton Longueville. The menu included melons, venison pasties, rounds of beef, chicken breasts, legs and shoulders of mutton, poultry, pullets with bacon, salted tongues coated with sugar and mustard, roasted apples, tarts, cakes, cider, ale and a variety of wine—all of which made our summer picnics of cucumber sandwiches and crisps a little dull.

The size of the Mere then was sixteen hundred square acres, and the depth of the water varied considerably depending on the season. In winter it often overflowed its banks, taking in much of the surrounding Fen and doubling its size. If it froze, it naturally became an attractive venue for skaters. Its waters contained 'an abundance of fish' including pike, eels, perch, carp, tench, bream, chubb, roach and gudgeon, so it was clearly an angler's paradise.

Its shorelines also made it a botanist's paradise because the banks and spinneys surrounding it were rich in wild flowers and ferns. John Clare frequently walked from Helpston to the Mere (which for him was beyond Yaxley and the Al) to look for rare ferns. When he was first taken to London and shown the River Thames, he was not at all impressed and said it had nothing of the grandeur and breadth of Whittlesea Mere. He was nothing if not loyal to his own, and neighbouring, countryside.

Other famous travellers and writers visited the place, and there are some graphic accounts of it in Lord Orford's *Voyage Round the Fens in 1774*. In those days it was usual for the banks of the Mere at regatta times to be crowded with sideshows, booths and amusements, very much like a fair, with hot sausages, pork pies, toffee-apples and drink. It even had a bandstand so that people who had come for a good day out could be entertained with suitable music. Celia Fiennes—that remarkable lady who toured England on horseback long before William Cobbett thought of doing so—visited the Mere in 1697. George Borrow also knew it well, especially from those days when his father was the commanding officer at the Norman Cross prisoner-of-war camp near Yaxley.

The Mere, as those people knew it, has long since gone.

Shrinking as it was with the drainage of the Fens, it was itself finally drained in 1851, when a newly designed Appold Pump (which had recently been on show at the Great Exhibition) was brought into use at the pumping station at Johnson's Point. Hundreds of spectators came from miles around to watch the water disappear. Some brought snacks, and some had handcarts to carry away whatever they could salvage from the mud. It revealed far more than they bargained for. As well as shoals of gasping fish and useless debris, they found the skulls of wild boar and wolves. From the mud also came the remnants of Ramsey Abbey silver, dumped there at the time of the Dissolution—a silver censer and a silver incense-burner, which were later sold for a considerable sum of money.

Today there is even less for us to see—at least on the surface. But stand there with a modern Ordnance Survey map and a copy of Bodger's map of 1786 and you can trace the shoreline of the old Mere. You will notice, too, that some of the names of the original creeks and landing-stages are preserved in the place-names of today. The highest point of the drained Mere now was once the deepest part of the water, where a barge once sank with its load of Barnack stone on its way from the Nene to Ramsey. The bandstand has gone and the stranded boats have long since rotted away, but the memory and the atmosphere of Whittlesey Mere still survive. A sudden swirl of dust from the fields will remind you of the storms which took people like King Canute by surprise, or the croak of a pheasant will awaken ancestral thoughts of wild geese arriving on your hunting-ground. On a summer's day you might even see some of the butterflies or ferns described by John Clare or stand in the golden light of the evening and, like the television camera-man, be amazed that such a modest stretch of England can still hold you rooted to the spot when you should be on your way home.

Not far away from the Mere is the famous Holme Fen Post which will also give you some idea of how much this land has shrunk since the Mere was drained in 1851. To crumble a handful of that soot-black soil through the fingers is to experience a physical contact with the earth that is unforgettable. It is to be in touch with antiquity, to feel the true history of the Fens. Driving home in almost any direction, you will more than likely see in the nearby fields a pile or two of bog-oaks recently hauled out of the still shrinking earth by modern tractors. In those grim-looking brutes, which have provoked many a farmer's wrath, lies the key to a totally different kind of Fenland story, to a time when this part of England was thick with forests. Some of the bog-oaks are thousands of years old and were already buried in the peat long before the pyramids were built in Egypt or the Chinese dynasties displayed their glories.

You might think that such comparisons need a little imagination. If so, be content to look across the fields to where the setting sun once reflected in the waters of Whittlesea Mere and you will feel that the events of its history are not so long ago, or beyond the mind's reach. Just beneath the surface are the hidden places, waiting to be reborn.

13 Milestones and Other Interludes

There is something very satisfying, even comforting, about travelling on roads that one has known for a lifetime, especially when some of those roads have changed hardly at all since I was last on them. And yet one can feel the presences of other travellers from far back. Beneath the uneven surfaces it becomes almost possible to see the footprints which were made in times long forgotten. There is a familiarity about each gate, each fence, each hedgerow or landmark which relaxes the stride, allowing the eye to scan those distances beyond the normally accepted limits.

Our roads and rivers have a compelling way of luring you into the Fens. They are usually so straight, so direct when they are the makings of man. Take the roads first. They may not be as full of surprises as the twisting roads you find in hill country but they can excite and draw you on to moments long anticipated as you travel towards a particular place.

One of the old features which I miss on our modern highways is the milestone. I realize that at the speed we travel now they would not be much use. At sixty miles or more an hour they can hardly be seen out of the corner of the eye and, where they exist, are usually lost in the overgrown grass verges or are crudely mutilated by hands which have no sense of the past.

Today's announcement of miles has to be much more practical and brazen. Our roads now are punctuated by towering blue or green boards which speed us on our way as though we were nothing more than cans of beans on some mass-production line. The boldness and size of our road signs are, of course, necessary but they can never have the same romantic appeal, as the old stone or iron mile-

'Roads and rivers lure you into the Fens'

posts of another age, each with its own individuality or quirk of the stonemason's hand. Having said that, I have to admit that some of the rural signposts (as distinct from milestones) can be very confusing, not infrequently contradicting the roads shown on the atlas and pointing us to places we do not wish to visit, whilst totally ignoring those places which we do.

Cambridgeshire can claim the introduction of the first milestones used in England since the Romans built their roads. In 1729 milestones were set up on the road between Cambridge and London and were paid for out of a local trust fund administered by Trinity Hall. The idea soon caught on, and by 1750 the rest of the country's major highways recognized the importance of using them.

Perhaps we should not be surprised at this. Cambridgeshire people like to believe that they are always ahead of the rest of the country in most things from agriculture to heart-surgery. Certainly by the middle of the eighteenth century travellers really thought they were making progress when they could join an express coach in Cambridge at four o'clock in the morning and be in London by seven o'clock in the evening. Each coach carried six passengers (all seated inside) and the fare in 1750 was 12 shillings return, which, by comparison with today, would have been at least the cost of a first-class rail fare. So the services were very much for the privileged few, for those busy and exclusive commuters of the day who were setting a new pace for life.

Travellers in less of a hurry, and with no right to such comfort, would catch the normal stage-coaches which were often over-crowded and more exposed to the weather. The sound of the post-horn and the teams of panting horses became a familiar pattern of each day. Similar journeys soon became commonplace from Huntingdon, Ely and Stamford, so the eastern region of England was not as isolated and out of touch with the rest of the world as we are sometimes led to believe. Progress had been made since the days of Hereward the Wake, and he, I'm sure, would have made the most of it.

Roads not only improved the prospects for travellers but also increased the opportunities for commerce. By 1750, for instance, three thousand brace of wildfowl a week were dispatched from Ely to London, and a livestock trade became profitable on most of the other stage routes in the country. East Anglia may not have been on the tourists' map then but it was providing London with many of the delicacies needed by the capital's eating-houses, such as wild duck, eels and skylarks.

It was, perhaps, not lack of roads which prevented people visiting the Fens two hundred years ago but the reputation of the weather and even that of the natives, both of which, as you know, are not deserved. Where could you find a more equable climate or gentler race of people, I ask? But what about the floods? And what about the Fen tigers? They are still there. Beneath the passive exterior the beast still roars, and some, I hope, will emerge from these pages. But, for a moment, I want to write about the visitors to the Fens.

In fact, when we look into the historical records we find that 'southerners' found their way in their thousands to Newmarket race meetings and to the Midsummer Fair at Cambridge more than 2½ centuries ago, some to try their luck with the horses at the one and some to enjoy themselves with the well-known ladies of easy virtue at the other.

The fair especially was then considered one of the largest and most attractive in Europe, with just about every trade being plied and every commodity on sale. People stayed for days, living on roast goose, roast pork, Colchester oysters and enormous quantities of ale. They played as long as they could, and slept where they fell. It has been estimated that as much as £250,000 changed hands in a week, a staggering amount of money for its time.

Public transport has always been a great benefit to local feasts and festivals. When the steam-engine replaced the stage-coach, and the railways shortened the journeys in England, fairs which were in decline were suddenly resuscitated by the day-trippers who took advantage of the new rail excursions. By 1859 Peterborough's Bridge Fair could expect ten thousand visitors a week to be brought to the city by the railway companies. We sometimes forget that the often modest and run-down fairs of today have such a lengthy and romantic past, a past which, in many cases, goes back for five hundred years.

But I must not digress. Roads and rivers are what I am supposed to be writing about, and when you can get away from the trunk roads, with their intimidating juggernauts, it is still possible to enjoy a peaceful drive through the Fens. Such roads often make it possible to get to a quiet stretch of river when the pleasure of walking can be renewed and an unspoilt world discovered. I am reminded of some lines by the poet Edward Thomas:

> Roads go on
> While we forget, and are
> Forgotten like a star
> That shoots and is gone.
>
> On this earth 'tis sure
> We men have not made
> Anything that doth fade
> So soon, so long endure. . . .

If roads can speak of history, so can rivers, as I realized from our week on the boat. The man-made waterways of the Fens, deprived of nature's flirtatious loops and meanderings, do not snake their course through the landscape as they do in the Yorkshire Dales or the shy valleys of Devon. They thrust themselves like billiard cues across the green tabletop of land which lies *below* their banks, and, in the evenings, they pot the setting sun as a snooker player sinks the last red ball before the black of night declares that the day's game is almost over.

They were not always so when left to nature. The original course of the Great Ouse was often referred to as 'the Bailiff of Bedford' because, when in full flood, it could force people out of their homes as if, in some unfortunate way, they had failed to pay their rent to the god of water. Cornelius Vermuyden helped to make their homes a little safer in the seventeenth century by his drainage systems, but it has taken a lot of effort and ingenuity since then to make our homes secure today. Already in this century, people have been flooded out of their houses by angry waters which not even modern engineering has been able to control.

Wherever there are rivers in the Fens, there is a threat that one day they will rise again, making their claim on a land which was taken from them. It is a fine balance between power and destruction. One can sense the danger poised like a tightrope-walker over the fields. Close the eye for a moment and the beast could leap.

But the rivers of the Fens, with all their threats, are still a compelling, dominant part of our country. As I sat by a placid stretch of the Nene one afternoon, I recalled days when the wind gave the surface of the water a cheese-grater roughness. I remembered days when ice slowly formed along the bank, halting the flow of history from the uplands to the Wash. I thought, too, of a walk I had taken along the same towpath, when spring made no promise of the days to come. The late afternoon sun was already behind me, casting its slanting amber light over the land to the east. Looking back, I could see white farm cottages ten miles away, dwarfed into insignificance against the great expanse of sky. Gulls fell and floated through the air like starched handkerchiefs snatched from a washing-line. Yes, in these days of washing-machines and airless launderettes, it is still possible to see a line of washing blowing in the Fens, and many a housewife still maintains that clothes are never cleaner than when they have 'had a good blow'. Shirts puff like overweight ghosts, sheets strain like spinnakers, and the multi-coloured knickers could even be mistaken for an urgent message from Nelson's flagship.

One of the great advantages in the Fens is that the roads and rivers often run parallel so that we have the twin benefits of two 'highways' leading to wherever we wish to go. I use the word 'highways' deliberately because Fen rivers are frequently higher than the roads. Strangers to these parts find it disconcerting to discover that the road on which they travel is overlooked by a river several feet above them, and, but for a solid, man-made bank, they would be washed away. But when that fear is overcome, you can then safely stop the car and climb up onto the bank, where your eyes, unaccustomed to such space, will be amazed at the scene before you. As we discovered from our week on the fenland waterways, a river-bank in the Fens is a vantage point. On a clear day you can see for more than twenty miles. Displayed before you will be a living atlas, a chequered pattern of fields, farms, droves, drains and clusters of sheltering trees, ordered and placed as though by an intelligent child's hand making its model world. Above you will be the benevolent, ubiquitous sky, the like of which you may not have seen before, and may not see again, so versatile is the hand that shapes our days.

In the early months of the year, before the days lengthen, or later, when the autumn brings night a little closer, it is a memorable experience to travel home on these river-roads. As the light begins to fade, the Fens take on that indescribable mystery which they so often acquire at twilight. Mist rises from the fields. A pheasant's cry adds its own ghostliness to the silence. You can almost feel earth stretching itself out to sleep.

Thinking of such quiet moments, I am reminded of an evening when I walked home at the end of a day spent between earth and sky, between light and dark. I had stayed out as long as possible, reluctant to separate myself from a world which satisfied every need. The far horizon to the east had already passed into night as I turned for home. By the time I had walked a mile or two along the bank towards the distant city, the setting sun was as red as a newly cut wound. As it slipped slowly from our world, it became elongated, an abandoned rugger-ball on the touch-line of the sky. Behind the drifting smoke of the brickyard chimneys, the last remnant of light blurred into grey cloud. Ahead of me the city lights became more clearly visible, more unreal and alien. As if to complete the day, a heron rose from the riverside and loped nonchalantly over to the opposite bank. Once again I felt that I was observing some strange, mythological bird rising out of the dim past, a prehistoric moment out of time venturing to show itself when no one was looking.

Herons fascinate me. They are, like skylarks, so much a part of the Fen country and seem out of place anywhere else. I have admired them since I was a child. I treat them still as god-like creatures that have survived all the changes and vicissitudes of the Fens. I look up in awe whenever one flies over. I slow down and hold my breath when I pass one on a river-bank. They have become sacred. I watched that solitary night-flyer as he settled on the other side of the river and became lost in the shadows. With his retiring into the dark I knew it was time for me to return to that world of artificial light.

14 A Roundabout Way to Wisbech

I always used to feel sorry that Wisbech was cut in half by that awful road the A47. The constant two-way flow of heavy traffic made it almost impossible to appreciate the attractions which the town still has, together with much evidence of its more prosperous past. With the additional traffic coming in from the north to join the A47, Wisbech got more than its fair share of noise. For many people it was simply a place to pass through as quickly as possible, and I must admit to avoiding it whenever I could. But now the West Walton Highway Bypass (which is part of the Birmingham to Great Yarmouth Trunk Road being built) has changed all that, and there are, in any case, other ways into the town for anyone not in a hurry.

It must be clear by now that, travelling west to east, Whittlesey is my natural gateway to the Fens, and so I set off for Wisbech along the north bank of the Nene, skirted the edge of my native town and took the road through Eastrea, Coates and Goosetree. The weather forecast had promised a hot day, and when I left home, the sky was blue and cloudless. But as I went deeper into the Fens, a dense mist flooded the land, and the distance was no more than a grey mouldy blur.

I took the road to Coldham and Friday Bridge, travelling slowly between chestnut and apple trees, until I reached Emneth. The haze added a mysterious quality to the summer day. Here and there two or three beet-hoers worked silently in the fields, the men already stripped to the waist, the women almost so, all anticipating the warmth that was to come. The rest of the fields were empty of workers, the crops waiting for the appropriate time of harvest. Machines have made the Fens even lonelier than they used to be. Only rarely do you see gangs of people working in the fields, and these you are most likely to see around Wisbech. But today only the beet-hoers brought movement to the land, their arms rhythmically chopping away, the ticking pendulums of a clock that measured their days in furrows rather than minutes.

The poppies which lined the roadside and dykes looked particularly luminous in the eerie grey light. On some of the headlands they were mixed with stray pieces of oil-seed rape still in flower. Trees appeared and disappeared like shadows. Cobweb pylons faded mistily into the distance, perhaps the only chance they have of looking beautiful.

I had forgotten what a fine Marshland church there is at Emneth and decided to pay it another visit. I could not have been more fortunate. Not only was the church open on a Monday morning, but it was also in the middle of a Flower Festival. As soon as I opened the door and stepped inside, I entered a world of lovely scents, colours, imaginative arrangements and stillness. The surprise increased my wonder and appreciation. It was one of the best displays I had seen for a long time, and there was not even a collection-box through which I could express my gratitude. The leaflet told me that Emneth means either 'the village in the meadows' or 'smooth meadows', and those descriptions seemed most appropriate at that moment.

'Cobweb pylons faded mistily into the distance'

From Emneth I made my way through Marshland St James, then on to St John's End and the Wiggenhalls—all four of them. Here one has the chance of crossing and re-crossing those great waterways which flow out to the Wash—the Middle Level Main Drain, the Great Ouse and the Relief Channel from Denver to Lynn. I went first to Wiggenhall St Mary Magdalen, a quiet, dreamy place on a misty summer morning where once the nuns of Fontevrault Abbey found their peace. In the distance I could see what appeared to be a ruined church and discovered this was Wiggenhall St Peter. I was told by a lady who was gardening nearby that, although the church was in such a ruinous state, it was not a redundant church. 'We do have a service there one day a year, on St Peter's Day.' I looked at the building and wondered how. There was no roof, windows or doors. Where the people once sat is now a congregation of small trees, bushes and weeds. A blackbird sang in the belfry, the only peal of bells heard by those stones for many years. And yet there was no gloom about the place. There was still a presence, a peace, which cannot always be found in churches that are well kept. But what a difference, I thought, between Wiggenhall St Peter's and Emneth's St Edmund's.

A very different experience awaited me at Wiggenhall St Germans. I had decided that, as it was a few minutes past midday, I would call at the Crown and Anchor for a bar-snack. I was amazed to see the pub so full at this hour on a Monday and assumed that it must be a very popular hostelry. When I went up to the bar to order my drink, I was a little puzzled to see a basket of various medicines and boxes of pills on the counter. One of the locals then explained to me that 'twelve o'clock on Mondays' was the doctor's surgery. ' 'E'll be 'ere any minute now if you want 'im to give yew a look over. That won't cost yew nothin'.'

I did not know whether to believe him or not, but, as I gazed round at all the people who were waiting, they certainly looked just like any crowd in a doctor's waiting-room—apprehensive, afraid, or mildly belligerent.

'Well, at least you don't have to go very far for your medicine,' I said, taking my first long sip of draught bitter.

'Not the sort you mean, me old beauty. 'E won't let us

have any of that stuff if he can help it. All he gives us is those damn' pills.'

At that moment the doctor arrived, in open-necked shirt and ready for action. The 'surgery' was held in a corner of the pub, just out of sight (but not out of hearing), and the first patient was called. One by one the villagers went in for their brief consultation, and slowly the pub emptied of all but the two or three fit and friendly drinkers. It seemed a perfectly satisfactory and amicable arrangement to all concerned and offered me a slice of local life I had not expected to find. It's a pity discretion forbids my telling more.

Those who were left started talking about a recent thunderstorm which had killed several people in Hertfordshire, some of whom had sheltered under a tree. 'I don't see how they can say that lightning were an act of God. I bet He don't know how many trees there are out there, so why should He decide that the lightning's going to strike one more than the other?'

I left them to it and walked out into the now bright sunshine. The mist had dispersed, the day was hot. I stood on the river-bank and looked at the wide stretch of muddy water flowing calmly towards the sea and remembered how violent it could also be. The cluster of small houses and red roofs made a pleasant scene, and I was pleased that my route to Wisbech was taking in so much of interest.

A short distance away is the Wiggenhall St Germans Pumping Station, one of the great protectors of the Fens. Its powerful pumps are capable of discharging over six million gallons of water a day and, during the disastrous floods of 1947, worked for nearly seven hundred hours non-stop. People who can remember those terrible March days of nearly forty years ago recall how the earth shook with the vibration of those engines working flat out, day after day, until one became fearful and apprehensive when they stopped.

If nature has not been kind to the Fens as a whole, it seems to have had a special grudge against Wisbech for the past eight hundred years. In 1236 it was severely flooded and hundreds of sheep and cows were lost. In 1260 most of the town was destroyed, including its fortified castle. Twenty-five years later the floods struck again and

'Wisbech, Elm, Tydd and Leverington were drowned.' In 1570 the famous historian Holinshed recorded that, 'There chanced a terrible tempest of winde and raine, the sea break in betwixt Wisbech, Walton, Walsoken, drowning Tilnie and old Lin.'

It must be remembered that the Wash coastline was much further inland than it is today and that Wisbech was an important port from medieval times up to the middle of the nineteenth century. The drainage of the Fens in the seventeenth century, and the rechannelling of the Great Ouse, eventually made King's Lynn the more important port but Wisbech still manages to attract considerable trade. In 1825–6 it handled 1,209 ships with a total cargo of more than 70,000 tons. The advent of the railways brought a decline in shipping trade for Wisbech, and the Second World War prevented any further development. Even so, the port today receives on average four hundred ships a year and handles well over 230,000 tons of produce, mainly grain, timber, animal feeds and fertilizers.

Flooding has always been a great threat in this area of the Fens, and I will write more about it in a later chapter. Having arrived in Wisbech, it is not tragedy I wish to consider now, but achievement, for the town has produced a few remarkable people in its time. Most famous of them all is probably Thomas Clarkson, who was born in 1760 and who became a passionate campaigner for the abolition of slavery. He was a Quaker and a great friend of William Wilberforce. He toured the country, urging the nation to oppose the atrocities it was guilty of in shipping slaves to the New World. Because of his service to humanity, he was made a Freeman of the City of London and, in a sonnet by William Wordsworth, was referred to as a 'firm friend of human kind'. Wisbech made sure that Thomas Clarkson would not be forgotten by erecting a sixty-eight-foot monument by Sir Gilbert Scott to his memory, at a cost of £2,035 in 1881.

Another Wisbech son who was to make his mark upon history was William Godwin, the philosopher, novelist and political thinker. He had trained to become a Presbyterian minister, like his father, but became instead an agnostic. In 1797 he married the writer Mary Wollstonecraft, mainly to protect the rights of his child she was bearing (who later became the second wife of the poet Shelley), and the family spent the rest of their tempestuous life in London.

A person who did more good for society than Godwin was Miss Octavia Hill, who was born in Wisbech in 1838. She was a philanthropist and reformer of living conditions for the poor. In 1856 she became secretary to the Educational Classes for Women at the Working Men's College, Great Ormond Street, and a few years later, with her sisters, started her own school. With financial help and advice from John Ruskin, they bought three more houses and began to train girls in home management. Her views and experience were soon called upon by the Church Commissioners, who asked her to manage several houses for them. But in Wisbech, and perhaps elsewhere, she is remembered mainly for her part in co-founding the National Trust, in 1895, along with Canon H. D. Rawnsley and Sir Robert Hunter. There is a plaque to her memory on the house where she was born on South Brink.

Several famous men and women have visited Wisbech, including Celia Fiennes, Samuel Pepys, Peter de Wint, William Cobbett and John Clare, who had hoped to find work there as a junior clerk in the office of Mr Bellamy, a local solicitor. Bellamy took one look at the scrawny young boy in his ill-fitting clothes and decided it would be in the interests of everyone to send him back to Helpston. Would we, I wonder, have had the poetry from Clare had he been acceptable as an office boy?

Because I have written of North Brink and Peckover House in previous volumes, I will not repeat myself here, but one cannot ignore that fine, elegant frontage or dismiss the days of prosperity which once made this town such a popular place and earned for it the title 'Capital of the Fens'.

Still avoiding the A47, I made my way home round by Tydd St Giles, Parson Drove and Thorney. It had been an impulsive decision which had taken me out for the day in the first place but, as 'the good book' says, 'Seek, and ye shall find', and I can't grumble at what I have brought back. Being a greedy person, however, I know I shall be back for more.

15 Many Shades of Green

The winds were those of a stormy March, the clouds were those of an unfriendly December, but the month was June. As I travelled along the empty road from Whittlesey to Benwick, only the land with its many shades of green convinced me it was summer. The sage-green of unripened wheat, the moss-green of potato crops, the almost copper-green of barley, the high-gloss green of the sugar-beet leaves (for which I can think of no other description than 'sugar-beet-green') and the sallow green of the dykeside grass all patterned the earth so abundantly that there was not an inch of black soil to be seen. The fields were full of growth. Trees struggled to hold on to the earth. The water in the dykes was corrugated. Everywhere there was movement. Acres of barley heads panicked like a shoal of frightened fish as the wind chased over the land. Poppies blew like red-hot sparks along the river-banks, and the larks were earthbound.

I continued through Doddington and Wimblington, through Manea, Tips End and Welney, then crossed the Hundred Foot Washes to Littleport. Gradually the wind began to subside and the exhausted clouds retreated, their herd-like anger spent, their stampede over. The more usual character of June asserted itself. The sky was suddenly blue, the air summer-warm, and the trees began to relax.

Earlier in the year, when we had spent our week on the Fenland rivers, I had noticed the Black Horse at Littleport and promised myself a visit there one day. This day seemed as good as any and, as it was already a few minutes past noon, I decided to look for the pub again. There was only one customer ahead of me. The landlady was doing her ironing at the bar, and I felt an intruder. After the usual courtesies (brief in the Fens), I ordered my beer and food, then sat in the quiet restaurant overlooking the Great Ouse. For late June I was surprised to find that there were no boats on the water and suddenly wished I could be out there again, enjoying the freedom of boat-travel, repeating the journey we had made in spring. A few swans went by, then a convoy of ducks. The wind, though gentle by comparison with an hour ago, was still strong enough to sweep the grass of the riverbank so that it had the texture of brushed cloth. From the window I could look across the water to the fields in Burnt Fen and recall our days on the River Lark and Brandon Creek. I wondered how the potatoes were looking which I saw being planted during those cold, early days in April.

As I ate my well-cooked lunch, I also thought of what a different world it is now from that which had known the Hunger Riots of 1816. Then the town of Littleport was, like many other East Anglian towns, seething with unrest and anger at the injustices they were facing. Men could not find work, their families were starving. Those who were employed had their wages reduced to 7 or 8 shillings a week, while the price of wheat rose to more than £5 a quarter. Survival was measured by the cost of flour and the value of bread.

There had already been uprisings at Southery, Brandon, Downham and Upware. It was becoming clear that for men who had little to lose there was a risk that they would take the law into their own hands. As Richard Rutter, who was one of the 1816 rioters, said at his trial: 'I decided I might as well be hanged as starved.' Rutter was one of the eighty rioters arrested and sent for trial at a special assize held in Ely, which lasted for a week. Twenty-four of the prisoners were sentenced to death, including one woman, but, following much public concern about further reprisals, only five men were eventually hanged. The rest, with several others who were arrested, were transported for life to Botany Bay. The families and the history of Littleport were changed dramatically by the events of that year. Now, nearly 170 years later, it is a different town as well as a different world. Even in our days of recession and high prices there is a prosperity which the Littleport martyrs

Swans on the Great Ouse

could not have imagined in all their dreams of revolution and luxury.

I left the Black Horse to make my way to Prickwillow, where I wanted to revisit the pottery shop. When my wife and I had called in April, an unusual pocket-watch stand had appealed to me and I always regretted not buying it. Several years ago I had been given a silver pocket-watch which had belonged to a friend who would have been ninety-five this year. I never wore the watch (having neither chain nor waistcoat) but occasionally propped it up on my desk, using a book or paper-knife to stop it falling down. A pottery watch-stand seemed the ideal answer, if they had one left.

The two ladies who were in the shop were friendly and helpful. One was busy dusting some newly baked plates, using something which looked very similar to the leather scourges used by penitent monks in the Middle Ages. I commented on the likeness and was told, 'Oh, we often use them for the same purpose.'

'I wouldn't have thought you could commit many sins in Prickwillow,' I said.

'You'd be surprised!'

After a few more good-humoured exchanges I discovered that the only crime one of the ladies would confess to was that she had not gone to church on Sunday but had stayed at home to look after her sick mother, who was in her nineties.

'Much more commendable,' I said. 'Much more Christian.'

'I suppose you're right,' she said, giving the plate another expressive whack. 'After all, what's a church? That's nothing more than four walls.'

Having made my purchase, I wanted to spend a few minutes on the banks of the Lark before leaving the village. The beckoning water sparkled. The distance called. Out there was a world I still needed to explore, a world I knew little enough about.

But my journey was elsewhere, and it was time to think of returning home. Before doing so, I looked in again at the Drainage Engine Museum to admire those majestic engines which had once helped to tame the Fens. Normally I am not in the slightest bit interested in machines but there was something about that Mirrless Bickerton which filled me with admiration, for it, its makers and its users, and the part they had all played in the history of Fen drainage.

I have always had a similar admiration for the way that Little Downham has maintained its links with the old Isle of Ely. It has a splendid village sign which proudly proclaims that it is 'Downham in the Isle'. Its church guide is also a model of its kind—well written and informative, it is worth every penny of its 20 pence. How many church guides open with such an arresting paragraph?

> As you drive, or better still cycle, along the B.1411 from the City of Ely, the view you enjoy of Downham explains its ancient name. 'Downham' means 'Settlement on the Hill', and it stands on that ridge of high ground which rings the Isle of Ely. For many centuries before the Fens were drained, Downham was one of the few places where men could dwell. Even today, a walk on a winter evening to the west end of the village will reward you with a memorable experience. As the sun dips down over the horizon, you will see right across the flat Fen into distant Norfolk and Huntingdonshire. Far from the landscape being dull and tedious, it has a vastness and a grandeur which are awe-inspiring. . . .

Jolly good, Downham! The reader gets to page eleven before the church itself is described in detail, and every page, before and after, is full of interest. The village was once the episcopal residence of the Bishop of Ely, and in 1251 Bishop Hugh was able to write of his 'Park' at Downham of some 250 acres.

As I left the village, I was able to see for myself the wonderful panorama on each side of the road. It was not a 'winter evening', and the sun was not 'dipping over the horizon', but it was an impressive sight all the same, reminding me again of what this landscape must have been like when it was no more than a series of islands in a sea of 'water, marsh and wilderness'.

The Downham guide also refers to another tradition of the Fens which we shall never see again—the 'stilt-men' or 'stilt-walkers'. Before the Fens were drained, it was a common sight to see men getting about the flooded land on tall stilts. In 1611 Isaac Casaubon, writing of Downham, said: 'There are few houses. . . . Yet it has more than 400 bulls and cows besides flocks of sheep. I was amazed when I saw one man on stilts alone with one little son tend 400 cattle.' Fenmen who went about their labours on these 'extended legs' quickly became known as 'Cambridgeshire Camels'. A good pair of stilts made out of the best ash would last for three generations, and many were kept as souvenirs long after the art of using them had died out.

Little Downham, California, Dunkirk, Pymoor . . . . all names I have seen and used before. Now they had a new significance as I drove home under a calm summer sky which had started out so ominously. In the late afternoon the fields were even emptier than before. Most of the men had gone home from their work, apart from one or two who were still beet-hoeing—as if they had got into a groove and didn't know how to stop. In the low, slanting light the pattern made by the many shades of green was even more noticeable. There was an air of quiet beneficence everywhere. The men and the machines, the skills and labours which have created this land deserved my admiration.

Perhaps it was appropriate that such a day should end in Peterborough Cathedral with a programme of words and music, called 'Tidings of Great Joy'. And yet, I asked myself, could such gratitude and praise be contained even within that great building? After all, as the lady in the pottery shop said, 'That's nothing more than four walls!'

Maybe, but like a good many people, I bet she would defend it within an inch of her life.

16 'Though Dynasties Pass . . .'

Within the span of little more than twenty-four hours I recently had three experiences in Cambridgeshire very different from my usual country ramblings. The first was a visit to Duxford Airfield with a party of schoolchildren, the second was to the Fitzwilliam Museum, Cambridge, and the third was a tour of the Cambridge University Library—all of which made me take a closer look at those things 'close at home' which we can so easily get complacent about.

Duxford Airfield was something I had often passed but never felt inclined to stop at, even though I had occasionally caught a distant glimpse of some of its showpieces. Only a week before I had seen the ostrich-plumes of red, white and blue smoke from the acrobatic Red Arrows decorating the Fenland sky and thought, 'One of these days . . .', but, as I usually prefer silence to noise, I do not go out of my way to look for aircraft.

This time, however, it was different, and the day came sooner than expected. As I made my way in the school bus along familiar roads, I tried to appear interested but still could not help wondering why I was going to this department of the Imperial War Museum just to look at a few archaic aeroplanes with twenty children who were all born well into the Jet Age.

The harvest fields were already ripening. A rash of poppies spread an epidemic of measles along the grass verge. Toothpick church spires pressed indentations on the tight skin of the sky, and every other road looked far more inviting than the one on which I travelled.

Eventually our coach pulled up at the barrier and we waited for clearance. It was like crossing a frontier into a foreign country. Indeed, for the children, the past we had come to study *was* a foreign country, and I found myself having to travel in my mind over a dozen boundaries between their childhood and mine.

The confused singing which had accompanied our journey gave way to impatience. 'Why are we waiting, Miss?' 'What have we got to look for, Miss?' 'When do we get our packed lunches, Miss?' But before any answers could be given, the uniformed security guard gave permission for the barrier to be lifted and we drove in.

Duxford was established as an airfield as long ago as 1911 and has a history which covers all aspects of flying, from those early days of aviation-pioneering to the prototype of Concorde, from Tiger Moths to Tridents, Junkers to Javelins, autogyros to Sea-Hawks. There were flying-machines to awaken the interest of even the most reluctant visitor—machines made from wood or corrugated iron to sleek models which looked as if they had been fashioned out of solid steel.

As we walked under the wings of planes that had dropped their bombs on Berlin, Dresden, Hiroshima and Nagasaki, I became aware of the sound of skylarks singing above the nearby runway and was reminded of something which the poet Edmund Blunden told me about his time in the trenches during World War I. During one particularly fierce battle, when shells were bursting all around, he noticed that a skylark was still singing above the gun-fire. It immediately reminded him of England and of village cricket, and he knew then what he was fighting for, why he so desperately wanted to survive and get back home.

Hearing the skylarks over Duxford, I thought again of that gentle English poet who wrote of war and nature and, at that moment, all the machinery of destruction surrounding us had a different meaning. The doodle-bugs, Dambuster bombs, guns and tanks all belonged to a period of history which had also given me my childhood in a relatively undisturbed countryside of the Fens.

As if transported back to the years of that Second World War, I remembered very clearly a moment which had been completely forgotten until I stood there on the tarmac at Duxford. It was in summer of 1943 and, as thirteen-year-old boys at our over-crowded school, we were being left in no doubt about the consequences, or duration, of that war. Our headmaster reminded us in assembly each morning of the need for utmost patriotism and secrecy. 'Look out, there's a spy about' was a catch-phrase we used in both the classrooms and the lavatories. Perhaps it had an even more immediate application to us then as boys as we hid furtively in St Mary's churchyard, savouring the first suffocating drags of home-made cigarettes, but it took its place with the other slogans of the day, like 'Dig for Victory', 'Save Waste Paper' and 'Beat Firebomb Fritz'.

But the incident which I recalled that morning was of a visit to an exhibition of model battleships put on by the Royal Navy in the British Legion hall. Later that day it was discovered that one of the models was missing, and the following morning we were lined up in the playground, where we were told that such a theft was an act of treason. The loss of that toy battleship could give the enemy all he needed to know about our defences. It was an act of betrayal which put our Navy at risk and jeopardized the lives of thousands of our men. If the boy responsible for taking it did not own up, then he was a coward and a traitor.

The playground remained silent. We stood for ten minutes or more while the headmaster paraded up and down our ranks looking at each boy accusingly, staring at him with the cold eyes of a firing-squad. Still no one spoke. The pocket battleship was not found in anyone's pocket, and the mystery remained unsolved. The Royal Navy did lose many life-sized ships during that war but I doubt if it was because one small, grey metal toy had been stolen from an exhibition of war equipment designed to inspire us to greater heights of patriotism. We were convinced that it was only a matter of time before we would be called upon to man the real thing.

However, I digress. Even so, because of that memory, I was able to look back more clearly at the tanks and planes and remember also some of the older boys who had gone from my school to become pilots, sailors, paratroopers and rear-gunners. When I saw the vulnerability of those tiny, cloche-like cabins in the bombers' tails, I shuddered at what it must have been like cooped up in one, with flak bursting all round and Messerschmitts zooming in for the kill.

When, during one of the educational talks, the children of today were shown the types of gas-masks we were given to wear in 1939, I felt like some ancient voice speaking from the Dark Ages as I told them how we used to put them on in school and then rehearse our mad scramble for the nearest air-raid shelter half a mile away. Once, one of our teachers decided that we should sing a few songs to while away the time. We must have sounded more like prehistoric animals wheezing in damp caves.

Emerging into the sunlight of Duxford, we hurried over to the elegant Concorde and then, at last, it was time for our picnic lunch, and the Second World War seemed lost forever in the past.

But even the past of that war was nothing compared with the past I was about to enter when, a few hours later, I walked into the Fitzwilliam Museum. Bronze Age man, Classical Greece and Ancient Egypt put another perspective on memory, and on our history. Perhaps we should all visit museums from time to time, to remind ourselves not only of the historical pageant of which we are but a brief part but also of the achievements of the past. We can so easily fall into the trap of thinking that the people who lived three or four thousand years ago were terribly primitive and moronic, with no artistic skills or aesthetic appreciation. Yet some of the drawings and carvings from 2,000 BC can leave one spell-bound by their beauty, of both form and composition. Have we progressed so much, we may then ask.

As captivated as I am by Egyptology and the world of Akhenaton, the two items which impressed me most on this occasion were the manuscript of John Keat's poem 'Ode to a Nightingale' and Beethoven's pocket-watch. The worlds of poetry and music brought together in an elegant room in Cambridgeshire, worlds which cross frontiers and know no boundaries and have never, yet, been destroyed by war. Did the composer's hand really hold that watch and the poet's hand really write that page? Through them we can, as Gerald Finzi used to say, 'shake hands across the centuries.'

In contrast with the touch-tempting but untouchable Chinese jade or Early English silver, I spent the next two hours in the University Library with members of the

King's College Chapel from the Backs

Peterborough Precincts Society who had been invited by the Librarian, Dr Fred Ratcliffe, to see something of the work which goes on there. As someone who has been guilty of contributing one or two titles to library shelves, I was suitably humbled to hear of the four to six million volumes housed in that library (give or take a hundred or two). I was equally impressed to learn that, if all the bookshelves were put end-to-end, they would stretch from Peterborough to Norwich. Any author might well wonder where his own slim volumes were in such company, and I felt like a moth trapped in the woodwork.

Out of all those books it was perhaps appropriate that we should be shown part of the Peterborough Collection (which used to be housed in the Cathedral Library), and, from the documents on display, I was enthralled to see the actual Royal Order written by James I for the removal of the body of his mother, Mary, Queen of Scots, from Peterborough to Westminster in 1612. At least we managed to keep the body of Catherine of Aragon. I'd miss her if she were ever spirited away in the dead of night or taken to another resting place.

All too soon it was time for us to re-cross the boundaries of history, to board the coach and travel back to the present. As we left Cambridge, we saw through the summer trees one of the loveliest architectural sights in Europe—King's College Chapel from the Backs, and, in a way, it epitomized all that I had been thinking about for the last twenty-four hours. It spoke of civilization, freedom, peace, learning, music and worship. It was a visible, timeless statement of man's aspiration and achievements.

As we made our way homewards along the edge of the Fens, the farmers were preparing for harvest, the village greens were suitably active (or inactive) with their leisurely games of cricket, and the England that Edmund Blunden and his generation wrote about and fought for was still ours to enjoy. The adolescent tantrums from over-paid tennis-players at Wimbledon seemed no more than a comic intrusion on such an English Saturday afternoon. The beer-can percussion accompaniment of modern World Cup Cricket could not even begin to compete with the charm and almost silent concentration of the games at Dry Drayton, Fenstanton or Godmanchester. While the fielders looked for the ball, the spectators might have looked up and listened to a skylark singing, or they might have noticed the bank of scarlet poppies and thought of their meaning for us now.

Our coach moved on, leaving each village scene to its own place in history, and it is reassuring to believe that these daily affairs in the lives of men and women will go on 'though dynasties pass'. At least we hope they will, if only commonsense and wisdom can prevail. After two such happy days I would not like to think that we were but fading characters in the last chapter of civilization.

17 Elegy for an Afternoon

More and more I realize how difficult, even impossible, it is to recapture the essence of a landscape from within the confines of four walls. A room shuts out more than sound, or space, or smells. It cuts off the heart-beat of the earth. The responses of the imagination become second-hand, even artificial.

Words, for me, have to be born out of doors, in the spaces which they are trying to describe and with the atmosphere they are straining to evoke. They may be worked on later, refined or polished, but their genesis has to be where the idea first struck root. It is necessary to stand and *look* at the earth and to feel the earth looking back watching each stroke of the pen upon the page, making sure that the line is as accurate as possible. There must be an understanding between the subject and the artist, a confidence which allows the truth to be told. The eye has to *listen*, the hands move blindly, as if guided by an extra hand. There has to be discipline and freedom. The eye must not leave its subject, for, in that split-second, a whole universe can change. It's a patience game. Sometimes one can wait all day for a sentence, for the words to bite. At other times it is difficult to catch them all, they come so abundantly.

I watched the land earlier today, each contour, each familiar feature, clear in my mind. The light was sharp, clean-cut, and the fields stretched neatly away towards a definite horizon. A foam of clouds blew across the sky, soap-suds of a summer's washing-day. There was no one to be seen. The Fens appeared empty or, rather, undisturbed by human-kind. The inevitable shimmer of lark-song gave an aura to the sky, and the river flowed lithely through dreamy banks.

And then I thought I saw the fields shrink back into themselves, tremble a little, shudder from their shoulders down to their buried toes, as if the change of wind told them something only they could know. The spell was broken. For once I could not even record my feelings on the spur of the moment for I had gone out into the Fens without notebook or pen. I felt frustrated, as a photographer must be without his camera when the shot of a lifetime is there for the taking.

I felt the air put on weight and become sultry. It was as if some invisible tide had turned. The horizon's clouds grew dark and as heavy as rocks. The light in the fields went out. A minute later and it began to rain.

I came home and sit now within these solid walls trying to call the morning back. All the words I wanted to use have fled, are lost somewhere out there where earth absorbs the seasons, years, failures, regrets, and all those unwritten sentences.

I console myself in a marvellous painting I have recently acquired of Holme Beach, by Ronald Crampton. I have never known a picture haunt me so much before. Four small figures at the edge of the sea, which appears to be always moving, always changing colour, as do the stormy clouds above. And yet, in this small painting, there is a stillness (as there is in all Crampton's work) which is mesmeric, which will not let you move until it has finished what it had to say. It cancels out time and makes the past and the present as one.

I have known many afternoons like it on those North Norfolk beaches of Hunstanton, Snettisham and Holme. They are all a long time ago now, before the Second World War cut short innocence, but I have old family photographs of when I played on the sands there, with no one else in sight. An empty beach with a deckchair and a pile of clothes. A pool of water left by the tide. Looking at this painting again is like rediscovering part of myself. I feel that, if I were to call out to one of those small figures within the frame, *I* would turn round to see who the stranger was calling from this far.

But do I want to disturb that child's absorption with his shallow pool? Am I still afraid of that cold, grey sea? Perhaps not so much now. Norfolk has been a favourite

'I saw the fields shrink back into themselves'

county since childhood and has meant even more to me during the last few years. It provides the 'still centre' when all around is turmoil. The air has a different quality to it the moment you cross the border. You can smell when you are entering Norfolk. There is a softness and a sweetness in the air.

I remember now that in those pre-war days one of the attractions of going to Sunday School was the prospect of the annual Sunday School Outing to somewhere in Norfolk. For a lot of the children in those days the Outing was their only holiday. The market-place would be packed with all the denominational contingents suitably branded with different coloured bows of ribbon pinned to jackets, shirts and dresses. Methodists, Baptists, Zionists, Congregationalists, Salvationists—hundreds of children and mothers herded together, waiting to be organized, waiting for the town band to head the procession down to the local railway station.

There were always calamities. More young Christian blood was spilt on that day than in the Roman Coliseum or Civil War. Children fought over possessions, broken spades, dented buckets or stolen sandwiches. Mothers fought over children, and Sunday School teachers fought over positions in the parade. On the crowded steam-train the children were handed packets of crisps and chewing-gum. Oranges and sausage rolls were taken from packed lunches and consumed before the Outing had gone three miles down the line. Two brothers, from a family well known for settling its domestic quarrels with a display of fists, took advantage of the confusion to settle yet another argument as to who was in charge of the lemonade. The language wasn't always what we were taught at Sunday School, and our fears grew that we would never all arrive in one piece at our destination.

Once, I remember, my mother could not come with us—probably because she had recently had another child—and so grandmother came instead. Tragedy struck almost immediately. A boy pushed me fully clothed into the sea, and grandma had to haul me out, drenched and howling, from the waves. More ignominy was to follow. I was taken up to a part of the beach where there was little shelter beneath the cliffs, stripped of all my clothing and wrapped in a coarse towel while my clothes were spread out to dry. I did not have a swim-suit and became the source of much giggling among the other children.

One year, this time on holiday with my parents at maybe Snettisham or Heacham, I remember standing alone on the wet, deserted beach. It was early morning, and I felt as if I should have gone out with the tide, as if I had been left on that glistening, muddy shore to evolve into something that could no longer claim the distant sea as its home. The beach bubbled silently with worm-holes, and razor-shells stuck out of the sand like broken shafts of Bronze Age spears. The distance, the space, the light and the blueness of the day over-awed me. Beneath the ever-watching sun I was on my own, to make of the world what I could. My parents, resting in the shade of the holiday chalet which they had rented, seemed equally far-off, as if they too belonged to another world. I was alone with the smells and the silence of an ancient kingdom which had no end even if there had once been a beginning.

But there was an end, not only to that day or that holiday but also to the experience of that child. I had to be gathered up, taken home, put back in the house and the street where I belonged. I had to go back to the crowded days of an ordinary life where the sounds and the smells were different. Even so, I feel that part of me is still there on that lonely beach at the sea's edge, waiting for the tide to turn, for the waves to reclaim me, for movement to come back into my limbs. Is that why Ronald Crampton's painting means so much to me?

On my way home from the Fens today I drove through Whittlesey and, beyond the veil of rain, heard the church bell tolling for someone's funeral. In the way that one memory has of unlocking other memories, I find myself now thinking of a funeral I attended as a small child. One of the girls in my Sunday School class had died, and we, somehow, all became part of the ancient ritual that saw her to her grave.

Her funeral took place one hot afternoon in summer. The entire Sunday School walked behind her coffin as it was carried through the town. The four bearers were, I believe, all uncles. I did not know it then but the feeling was not unlike that of being part of some half-forgotten Greek tragedy. The small girl could have been a child-queen mourned by her people. The shops were closed, the streets lined with silent, weeping faces. The procession moved with a calm, simple, primitive dignity, not in step but with a slow, rhythmic shuffle which gave the long line some order. The child's parents walked immediately behind the coffin, followed by other members of the family, all in deep mourning, their audible grief rising and fading through the afternoon like an ancient chant. Behind the family walked the Sunday School class—the girls in white dresses and the boys in white shirts, all carrying a single white flower. In the dry July sunlight our white dazzled in contrast to the black suits of the grown-up mourners, and our smaller footsteps added a syncopated echo to the tread of the adults. In the background the church bell was tolling. People stood on the edge of the pavement watching us pass. Out-of-work men took off their caps. Women cried and muttered things like 'Bless her little heart.' Then someone near the front of the cortège started singing:

Around the throne of God in Heaven
Thousands of children stand,
Children whose sins are all forgiven,
A holy, happy band. . . .

Slowly others started to join in, and soon we were all singing that sad, triumphant hymn as we made our way down Market Street, Eastgate, and then into Cemetery Road. I felt lifted on a wave of emotion that thrilled me. It was a sensation never experienced before. At this pitch I wanted the funeral to go on forever. Why couldn't days like this happen more often? This was even better than Christmas, or holidays. This drama had more ceremony.

It was only when we threw our flowers into the grave, and the preacher dropped some gravel noisily onto the lid of the small coffin, that I realized that we would never see this girl again, never share with her the model Garden of Gethsemane, or hold hands during prayers. She had gone, was lost, drowned under our wilting flowers and the mound of earth. Somehow, out of that darkness, out of the hole, she was 'going to be with Jesus', and I didn't understand how she was going to manage that.

For a town with nothing better to do on a July afternoon the event was over. We walked back to our houses, to our narrow streets where nothing ever happened, and the church-bells began playing 'The Bluebells of Scotland'.

The connection between the Sunday School Outings in Norfolk and the funeral is understandable. What is more interesting to me is how someone else's painting can unlock such a sequence of memories and make them all relevant to an afternoon.

I may not have written today what I had intended to write, but out of the earlier loss has come something which, for me, has more than compensated for the chapter which I had hoped to get out of the day. It evokes the spirit of the Fens as much as any description of a landscape could have done. As I said earlier, the Fens are not only fields and farms but people, and the people with whom I grew up have given my love of the Fens a quality it would not have otherwise had.

I am reminded of something which Laurens van der Post wrote in *Journey into Russia*: 'One never really knows another country unless one knows it through the life of the individuals who compose it.' As much as I like to present my own attitudes towards the area, in whatever I write, I know that my feelings are influenced by the lives of others who have a far more intimate knowledge of the place than I. One pair of eyes is never enough.

18 A Touch of Paradise

When I began this book, I did not know that I was going to write about so many octogenarians, but, understandably, they are the people who can still recall what the Fens were like nearly eighty years ago and I am grateful for their memories.

My latest discovery is Mr Henry William Dean, who was born in Cambridge in 1901. As with the other people of his generation whom I have met, his lively energy, conversation and sprightliness belied his years. He wasted no time in demonstrating to me the correct way of jumping a dyke—which is sideways and not like a hurdler—and by the end of the three-hour morning, I could fully understand why this self-taught, self-made man had made such a success of his professional life as a chartered surveyor.

But before we talked about his long associations with the Fens as an agent for several prominent landed estates and farm owners, I asked him to tell me about his childhood. In particular I wanted to hear of the summer holidays he spent 'in the country' with his grandparents.

'I remember them as clearly as if they were yesterday,' he said. 'We used to go by train from Cambridge to Six Mile Bottom, walking the four miles to Willingham Green, where my grandparents lived, which was midway between Brinkley and Carlton. Later we made the journey from the station by bicycle, or hired the village carrier to fetch us with his pony and trap. The thing I always noticed, even as a child, was the colour of the countryside. There was always such a profusion of wild flowers, wild roses, poppies, cowslips, toadflax and flowers you never see today. The fields were smaller too. Not the great hedgeless prairies you get now. In those days the fields all had hedges round them. And they all had names. It gave the countryside so much more identity. Made each plot more personal. Of course the roads were not made up then as they are now. They were mostly loose granite surfaces and rough droves which went down to the farms. The high hedges used to be full of birds' nests, and I have to admit to doing my share of birds-nesting. Do you remember how we used to take one of each species from the nests, piece a little hole at each end of the egg with a pin, then blow them to get rid of the insides?'

I remembered very well and was always amazed that out of such a tiny hole one could blow the contents of the egg to splash upon the ground, leaving the empty shell almost perfect.

'Getting back to wild flowers,' said Mr Dean, 'I remember how the local village children used to gather great bunches of them for decorating the church at Easter and Harvest. We used to have wonderful displays of produce and all the windowsills would be decorated with wild flowers and fruit. . . . Other things we took for granted then were the church, the village shop, the smithy and the carpenter's shop. I used to love going into the carpenter's shop because he did all his own painting of the waggons and would always try out the colour on the back of his shop door—reds, greens, yellows, blues—brush after brush had applied its own colour to the door so that it looked more like a rainbow. Sometimes he would cut off a chunk of the paint for me to take back home. I used to think it was beautiful.'

I remembered the smithy and the carpenter's shop of my own town. I also remembered the door of the old wash-

'There was always such a profusion of wildflowers'

house at the bottom of our garden which had been similarly coloured by my father trying out his paint-brushes.

Mr Dean then spoke of how he enjoyed playing with the village children, in and out of the stables, hiding in the mangers or going off to the fields, bridle-ways and woods.

'I used to love riding on the back of the horse that was taking a tumbril load of sheaves of corn back to the stackyards and then leading the horse back to the fields.'

'Were the harvests of those days as idyllic as we now think of them?'

'I think so. I'm sure people were happier in their work then, especially at harvest time. If it was a good harvest, they knew they'd be all right for the rest of the year. It was a time of celebration and thanksgiving. At the end of the harvest, when they all gathered together in the barn for their 'horkey'—which means Harvest Supper—they used to dance and sing. You could see gratitude in their eyes.'

I mentioned that John Clare often wrote of how the ploughman and field-workers sang at their work, and asked Mr Dean if he could recall anything like it.

'Oh yes. You could always hear men singing, especially at harvest-time when they had a break for their beer. There would always be someone with an accordion to start them off. I can also remember sampling some of that delicious home-brewed beer as well. There used to be an eighteen-gallon barrel for the grown-ups and a nine-gallon barrel of small beer for the children.'

'Why was it called "small beer"? Was it because of the size, or its strength?'

'Its strength, mainly. It wasn't as strong as the beer drunk by the men, not quite as potent.'

'Is that where we get the term "small beer" from when we refer to something which is not quite of the best?'

'Could be. . . . Certainly the beer the men had was good and must have boosted their strength. I've seen a man carry a sack of wheat weighing 2¼ hundredweight on his back more than once, and go up a ladder with it.'

There were many more memories of those far-off childhood summers to talk about, but I was anxious to hear also of how Mr Dean had become so involved in the farming life of the Fen country, how, from his modest beginnings and leaving school at the age of fourteen, he had become a Fellow of the Royal Institute of Chartered Surveyors, a Member of the Central Association of Agricultural Valuers and a Commander of the Royal Victorian Order.

'How do you achieve anything in this life?' he said with a smile. 'Hard work, fairness and a determination not to let yourself down. When I started work in 1916 as an office boy to the late Mr John Evans Bidwell, I made up my mind that I would not be satisfied until I had a firm of my own. When I left the Church of England school, I was helped considerably by the Reverend Canon Claude Essex, who became my mentor and friend for sixty years. He encouraged me to continue my education in the evenings, both through attending evening classes and taking correspondence courses, inspired always by my parents, who made considerable sacrifices for me to pursue my ambition. From 1919 to 1923 I studied for the examination of the Surveyors' Institution and the Auctioneers and Estate Agents' Institute. I went on courses, did field work and generally gained as much experience as I could.'

Such effort and determination did not go unrewarded. Mr Dean gained all his qualifications and, on 28 February 1930, at the age of twenty-nine became the manager of the firm he had started work with fourteen years earlier as a 'general office-boy and stamp-licker at 5 bob a week'. Six years later he became a partner of Bidwell & Sons and eventually, in 1949, he established his own practice in Cambridge, which is now run by his son, John Dean.

His work consisted largely of the management of estates in various parts of England, farming, valuations, sales, purchases, town-planning, rating, taxation and consultation. He has served as a Commissioner for the Middle Fen and Burnt Fen, and Mildenhall Drainage Boards. Among his many other appointments he has been on the panel of arbitrators for the Ministry of Agriculture, Fisheries and Food and conducted public enquiries for the Minister of Education.

I asked him why he had chosen to work so closely with farming.

'I just wanted to be in touch with the soil. I love the smell of the countryside, the feeling of growth. I loved nothing better than to walk through the corn or hayfields, or into a field of sugar-beet to part the huge leaves wet with the dew to see the size of the beet and then smell the sweet black earth below. It was the same with celery. Is there a more evocative smell than a field of celery in the early morning? I'd do anything to get out into the fields to experience moments like that. And one good thing about so many Fenland fields is that they are always well away from the roads. You can only get to them by the droves, so you get away from the noise of traffic, and when you walk down those droves, you have the feeling that you are walking into infinity.'

'It's a good job you didn't decide to become a writer as well,' I said, 'otherwise I wouldn't have had anything to write about.'

I then asked Mr Dean to give me his definition of a Fenman.

'All the Fenmen I've ever known have been hard workers. They never dawdle over their work. They get on with it. I also think they are a very resourceful breed. Mind you, I wouldn't give them many marks for humour. They were not called "Fen tigers" without good reason. They are a dour, rugged lot, with an in-bred defiance that some people find frightening. I never found Fenmen frightening, but I did realize that you have to win their confidence before they'll tell you anything. They don't give much away. I think it's because they spend so much time walking against the wind! They think everyone's against them to begin with, but when you get to know them, you can't meet a kinder, more generous set of people anywhere. And I think the old traditional farm foreman was the best of all. He had the gift of knowing the seasons, of knowing the crops, the land and his men. He was paymaster, overseer, seven-days-a-week-man, who always seemed to go about his work in a semi-trot instead of walking. The backbone of the Fens.'

I agreed enthusiastically with all that Mr Dean had said and talked for a few minutes about some of the farm foremen I had known twenty-five years ago, characters and individuals every one, who took tremendous pride in their work. Their fields were there for the whole world to see, and they had to look perfect, winter and summer.

The conversation turned to the seasons, and I asked if the summers were as hot as older people always say they were, or the winters as hard.

'Of course memory can play tricks on us, and we may forget those things we no longer wish to remember, but the summers were long and hot, with skylarks singing high above us, of that I'm sure. I can seldom recall it raining during those childhood summers we've been speaking of. Each year had a touch of paradise, something special. The winters were equally hard, and I have seen carrots dug out of the ground with a pick-axe. There was much more skating in those days too because the flooded fields would know weeks of frost. Yes, the seasons were—what shall I say? more definite.'

Already three hours of the morning had passed and there were still many other matters to discuss—Fen-blows, soil-shrinkage, the future of farming in the Fens, conservation and the Common Market. But it was lunch-time, and Mr Dean's daughter, the artist Tessa Beresford, thought it might be a good idea to have a stroll in the garden and then something to eat. Leaving the spacious house, we walked into the secluded garden at the rear of an old thatched barn and enjoyed the sweet air of the day. The newly cut grass gave off its own unmistakable smell, over-powering the more subtle scents of roses and flowering bushes. A thrush came down onto the lawn to sing for us. The sky was a pale, larkspur blue. At that moment I realized again how lucky I was to have a job which placed me in such a beautiful setting and allowed me to meet so many interesting people.

When we returned to the house for lunch, I discovered that Mr Dean had another passion in life—good food (with claret, port and champagne high on his list). He talked of his favourite restaurants in London, where to get the best lobsters or the best cheese, and then told me something else I did not know—that the Rose and Crown at Wisbech used to have one of the finest cellars in East Anglia and undoubtedly some of the best port in the country.

'I haven't been to the hotel for years now but it was always a visit to which I looked forward with pleasurable anticipation. You must go there one day to see what it's like.

The annual meeting of the Wisbech District Agricultural Valuers' Association was held there, and after lunch we used to have a little "flutter" by each putting half-a-crown in a bowl and then guessing what vintage was being served that day. Whoever got the year right collected the bowl of money. I was lucky enough to get it on one occasion, but the older members were far more knowledgeable.'

My pleasure in meeting Mr Dean had been greater than I had anticipated, and I drove home from his daughter's house in Hemingford Abbots knowing that I had been in the presence of a man who had enjoyed life abundantly. I knew also that he had done so mainly because of what he had put into it in the first place.

'I admire above all else', he said, 'hard work and the satisfaction it gives. . . . Hard work in all walks of life, and hard workers.'

Since that conversation with Mr Dean, I have been reading some back copies of the Wisbech Society's Annual Reports, and in the one for 1950 I was delighted to find an article on the Rose and Crown by A. A. Oldham and E. J. Rusdale. They certainly confirm what was said about the inn's fine cellar: 'The modern development of the hotel may be said to have begun under Mr William Tidnam, who took over in 1857. Later, his son Harry Augustus Tidnam was a great connoisseur of wines, and his advice was often sought by Continental vineyards. He succeeded in building up a great reputation for his cellars of Ports, Clarets, Burgundies, and Rhine wines, which became famous all over the country. . . .'

The history of that one Fenland inn could more than fill a chapter, for it has occupied a place in Wisbech for over five hundred years. One of the most traditional pictures to emerge from the Society's article is of those days when the Rose and Crown was the principal coaching-inn of the town. In 1792 the London Mail-coach ran daily to and from the Golden Cross at Charing Cross, and a coach called the *Hero* went each weekday from Wisbech to the White Bear in Piccadilly, taking 12½ hours for the journey.

Did someone like Mr Dean occasionally make that journey just to taste the best lobster or cheese the city could offer? I think I would have settled for a local cheese and spent the coach fare on an extra bottle of good port at the Rose and Crown.

19 A Love of the Land

A man who would agree with Mr Henry Dean about hard work is Mr Henry Beusch, one of the most determined and industrious men I have met.

Henry is a nurseryman in the Lincolnshire Fens and lives near Gosberton Clough. He has just one acre, and it's all under glass. When he showed me round, I was impressed by the orderliness and careful programming of his year's work. Because of the quick growth encouraged by the almost tropical heat of the glasshouses, there is always a job to do, each hour of the day, seven days a week, from dawn to dusk. Henry and his wife, May, do practically all the work themselves, growing everything from seed, grading and packaging the plants for other growers or the markets. I have to admit that cauliflower is not one of my favourite vegetables but I did experience a certain pleasure and amazement when I was taken into one of the houses to see 400,000 of them growing—and *they* were the third crop in that house within the year.

'You have to make the land work as hard as you do these days,' Henry said. 'Apart from when I am having the soil sterilized, there is always something growing.'

Life has never been easy for Henry Beusch. Born in northern Germany in 1925, he was conscripted into Hitler's army as a teenager, taken prisoner by the Allied Forces in August 1944 and brought to England, where, like many other POWs, he was put to work on building roads in Leicestershire. But as soon as the opportunity came, he volunteered to work on the farms. One of those days is still very clear in his memory.

'I remember it was on my twenty-first birthday, 7 April 1946, that I was planting potatoes, and it was snowing.'

'Had you worked on the land before?'

'Yes. Where I came from in Germany was much like this. My father died before I was born but my mother used to milk the cows and I had worked with cattle. A love of the land is born in you. You can't get away from it. I liked working on the farms in England and made some good friends after a while.'

'Why were you still a prisoner of war in England when the war was over?'

'Sometimes I think we were kept here as cheap labour and because we were such good workers. Besides, there was nothing for most of us to go back to in Germany. The country was ruined. I had the chance of being repatriated at Christmas 1947 but I liked it here and decided to stay. People in England still enjoy the best freedom in all the world, but they don't always appreciate it.'

Eventually Henry was sent to work in the Spalding sugar-beet factory. He was strong, weighed eighteen stone and spent most of his time carrying sacks of sugar that weighed as much. 'I could throw an eighteen-stone sack of sugar over my head as though it were as light as a pillow.'

But one day there was an accident and he suffered a serious back injury. No one realized at the time just how serious it was but it resulted in a tubercular spine and fifteen months strapped to a hospital bed. In all, Henry was out of work for five years because of his accident. His weight dropped from eighteen stone to seven, and his height was shortened by nearly four inches.

'The doctors told me I would never work again, and probably never walk again. But I couldn't accept that. I didn't want to live on the State. I wanted to prove I could work. So I renovated my own cottage. I did it all myself. I was still in a stocking-plaster from my armpits to my ankles and could not bend. I plastered the walls lying on my stomach because I could only move my arms upwards. I even put on the roof by myself. I've always been a determined person and would never let life get me down. Five years later I built my own bungalow, and furnished it, for less than £1,000.'

Seventeen years ago, having worked very hard for others, Henry decided it was time to start working hard for himself and so bought his own nursery.

'It was hard work right from the word go, and many times we put in an eighteen-hour day. My wife worked as hard as me. She's often out there even now at daybreak and doesn't finish until it's dark.'

'Why do you do it?'

'I sometimes ask myself that. When I go to bed some nights, I say "What am I doing this for?" Then I wake up in the morning and look out of the window and see all the things growing, and I don't need to ask any more. You can see what you've done the day before, and you know what you are going to do that day.'

He looked at his watch. 'Have you got time for a drive around?' I said I would like that.

We went down narrow droves where the ripening wheat almost brushed the sides of the car. The low light of the early evening gave the crops a golden warmth and stillness.

'How many acres of corn are we looking at now?' I asked.

'About two thousand. Maybe a little more.'

'The crops all seem to be in excellent shape. Is it going to be a good year?'

'No. All the crops are far too good for anyone to make a lot of money this year. When there's a glut of anything, it's not easy to sell at the right price.'

'Does the land around here fetch good prices?'

'The best land will go for £4,000 an acre or more.'

'I've noticed that the dykes are very empty and dry. Do you ever get drainage problems?'

'The land is over-drained and most of the field-dykes are neglected. I have seen scores of dykes disappear since I've been here. It's a mistake.'

We stopped at Kingston's Bridge Pumping Station to look at the water levels in the drains and South Forty Foot. In the clear light we could see buildings twenty miles away. The dyke-sides were thick with poppies. The air above us trembled with skylarks. It could not have been a more peaceful and satisfying evening.

We then made our way over Hundred Fen and Quadring Fen, and I could not help thinking that there were even fewer trees out there than in the Cambridgeshire Fens. One thing which was different was the soil. It was lighter and

Reed-cutting in the Fens

finer compared with the peat soil in the south.

'Which season of the year do you like most, Henry?'

'I love spring, and the smell of spring. You can't explain to townspeople what it's like, and they'd never understand. You have to be up early in the morning for one thing, but that's what I like best, the smell of an early spring morning, when everything's fresh and new.'

We drove on a maze of narrow roads, sometimes private roads, certainly roads I had never travelled on before.

'You must wonder where I'm taking you,' he said as we turned down a dusty track between two fields of potatoes. 'Don't worry. I know this area like my own jacket pocket. I could ride around like this for hours, just looking, and each time it's different."

As Henry had become a naturalized British subject in 1964, I felt I could ask him to express his opinion on England, and the English.

'As I said before, England is a good country where people can enjoy freedom. When I first came over here, I thought that British people were very honest. You could leave anything lying about and it would still be there at the end of the day. They are not so honest any more. And they will leave all their litter about. I can't understand that. When you have a beautiful country, why make it ugly with all the litter? It's bad enough in the streets, but when they bring it out to throw in the countryside, I get angry.'

We made our way back through the village of Gosberton Clough, paused to look at the tiny church of St Gilbert and St Hugh, where Henry and May worship each Sunday, and reached the house just as a huge red sun appeared from behind a cloud.

'You should have been here last night. There was the most magnificent sunset. The sky was crimson. That's what I like about these flat lands. You can see the sun get up in the morning and you can see it go to bed at night.'

Taking a last look round the glasshouses and the fruits of this man's work, I could not help remarking that it must seem, at times, a long way from that day when he planted potatoes in the snow and wore a prisoner's uniform.

'Yes, it is different now. It was not easy to begin with. People did not make me feel very welcome, which is understandable. But there is one thing about Fen people: they respect hard work. When they saw I was a hard worker, it didn't matter where I came from. I was one of them. Now I have many friends around here, and they would do anything for me.'

I left Mr Henry Beusch to lock up his world for the night and made my way back over the Lincolnshire Fens towards Spalding. I did not go right into the town but turned onto one of my favourite roads home—the Deeping High Bank to Crowland. Riding several feet above the level of the fields and the broad stretch of the River Welland I had a memorable view of the countryside with which to end the day. The fields in Deeping St Nicholas Fen had a red ochre tinge to them as the last half of the sun rested on the horizon. Beyond the river on my left was the unmistakable shape of Crowland Abbey. What a different world it was now from when that was built. And yet it had survived, had been determined to survive and would still be there when the world belonged to someone else and other crops waited beneath the sun. And who will love the land then? Who will be grateful for the smell of spring?

Seven weeks were to pass before I visited Mr Beusch's nursery again, and I was amazed to see that the glasshouse in which there had been 400,000 cauliflowers was now more like a tropical forest of cucumber plants roof-top high, with huge, rough leaves partly hiding the fine crop of dark green cucumbers. Henry had already taken five thousand of them from that one glasshouse alone, and he expected to crop at least fifteen thousand before they had finished.

I expressed my surprise at such growth and my admiration of such magnificent specimens, but neither gave much consolation to the grower, who was clearly disappointed in the price that he was receiving from the markets.

'You couldn't grow better cucumbers than that, and yet I'm getting less than 5 pence each for them, which is a fifth of what they're asking for them in the shops. Out of that I have to pay handling charges and transport, so you don't need me to tell you how I feel. It's a lot of hard work for very little. I have put in seventy-two hours this week, including two trips a day to the Leicester market when I don't get home until midnight. Then I still have to get up early next morning to start all over again. Nature, whatever it's growing, won't wait for you. Everything has to be picked when it's ready.'

'But it seems to me that you thrive on hard work, don't you?'

'I've always been used to it from when I was a boy. On the farms in Germany we worked 106 hours a week, including my mother, who started milking at 5.30 each morning and who still had the family to look after when she had finished her day's work. So I don't suppose I should grumble now, should I? I can't go on strike or on the dole, but I am my own master. I know who and what I'm working for. And, who knows?' he said with a smile. 'Next year the prices may be better.'

We finished the tour of the other glasshouses, all similarly transformed into a jungle of cucumbers or tomatoes, and made our way back to the house. A cool wind was now blowing in from the west, and there were all the makings of another dramatic sunset taking shape on the horizon. A fierce yellow light broke through at one point, and the outer rim of clouds began to redden like coals before a blacksmith's bellows.

'Come into the house and let's have a talk.'

By the time I left for home, the sky was dark, the sunset over and the fields had settled down for the night. The only lights to be seen were the little amber squares from cottage windows scattered like glow-worms over the earth.

There was a deep sense of contentment, achievement and purpose. Whoever comes to love this land, in spring or any season, will owe something to men like Henry Beusch who have a love for the soil which cannot be measured in market prices.

20 'Hurrahing in Harvest'

I always feel a little disappointed, even unhappy, if I am away too far from home during harvest time. Having watched the fields ploughed, having seen the drilling and the growing, I do like to be around when the crops are finally gathered in, to see the year's cycle completed. Not that I do anything but look on in admiration. I hardly know one end of a combine-harvester from the other, but I do get a tremendous satisfaction from seeing all those acres of corn and barley yielding their annual returns. We may no longer flock to church or chapel to sing 'Bringing in the sheaves. . . .' but the old traditions of harvest do survive both modernization and Mammon, and the feelings of gratitude and thanksgiving are, I'm sure, still there.

So, although it was holiday time, we had not gone too far away for me to feel deprived of this important ritual, and, with the harvest starting so early, I was able to see the cutting begin in Cambridgeshire, follow its progress through Norfolk and Suffolk, then re-cross the boundaries back home again to watch the last gatherings in the Fens. The experience will, I know, make all the difference to the winter months. The sense of pride and achievement will make the year whole.

Perhaps there is a deep-rooted awareness of such a continuity, a link with the past which conjures up a similar response in most of us. Even townspeople (forgive the expression) who profess no love of the country life seem to stir a little at harvest scenes, reflecting maybe on the thought that we were all countrymen once. The years pass, the new generations may dilute those old customs with their own life-styles, but we can never totally forget our debt to the land or the knowledge that our earliest forefathers lived close to the soil.

Apart from any traditional or historical associations with harvest, I simply love the season for its own satisfying sense of completion. I like the smells and sounds of harvest. Even the corn stubble has a glow and a texture which delights—that is, if you can get near to it before it is turned into a raging inferno. Yes, and even then (rightly or wrongly—and I believe wrongly) one feels that the burning of the stubble is part of the final sacrificial act to end the season. After the sophisticated technology used by today's harvesters, this last deed looks strangely primitive, if not barbaric. There is something menacing in the crackle of the flames through the straw. One expects the earth to scream out with pain, like some martyr from the Middle Ages.

Some years ago it was my privilege to take Helen Thomas—the widow of Edward Thomas—out for a car drive. She was then in her last years and almost blind. Although her sight had gone, her sense of smell was not impaired. 'Someone', she said, 'is burning corn stubble.' I looked around but could see no fires anywhere. But she was adamant. 'I think it's a dreadful practice,' she said with some vehemence. 'Don't they stop to consider all those innocent creatures in the fields?' We drove on for another half mile and turned a corner. There it was—the fire and the smoke, the fear and the terror. It was like watching a city being burnt to the ground.

In recalling that memory I am also reminded of a more recent conversation I had with Michael Stagg, Warden for the Suffolk Heritage Coast. 'Yes, it's frightening', he said, 'when you see such vast areas of the land burning. I feel we should all lament when we see the funeral pyres of the barley fields.'

Michael could, I think, be described as a poet of conservation. He has a sensitive, elegiac way of describing the passing of a countryside which may never be reclaimed. 'In ten years I have seen the county of Suffolk transformed as large areas of heathland have disappeared, mostly under the plough. It's like seeing a whole family, or generation, wiped out.'

When he spoke of his favourite river, the Alde, he referred to it as 'the plaintive river, the voice of Suffolk', and when trying to demonstrate the task of turning the tide of pollution, the tide of apathy, he could liken it only to the helpless King Canute trying to turn back the sea.

'I wonder what John Clare, or Edward Thomas, would make of our countryside now. What we are doing is worse than Enclosure. We are destroying a thousand years.'

It would, however, be unfair to put all the blame on the farmers. Some may be full of self-interest and want to get as much out of their land as they can, but I know quite a few who are 'conservation minded' and have spent a lot of money in planting hedges and trees in an effort to 'put something back', rather like Eric Slote.

A more pleasant sound which gets through the dusky haze with renewed poignancy is the screech of swifts in flight, reminding me not only of the street where I was born but of all the summers I have enjoyed. Last summer was no exception. We were staying at a friend's house in Suffolk and it was warm enough to sit out in the garden long after sunset, talking idly away under a pearl-grey sky which had not seen a cloud since Noah's rainbow promised the world it would never be flooded again—a story which some Fenmen accept with the proverbial pinch of salt. As we sat quietly watching the light change, a pack of swifts swirled in a great frenzy above us, sometimes spinning in a roulette of air, sometimes swishing through the sky like a quiverful of arrows released at Agincourt. Their presence took my mind back once more to that narrow street where I had spent my childhood, back to those summer evenings when my mother took us out gleaning in the fields between Whittlesey and Ramsey. We had waited, it seems, for days for the last cart-load to leave the field before we were allowed in to fill our sacks. But what a joy it was, and what a thrill to be out so late at night with that vast stillness surrounding us. It was an even greater thrill to watch a full moon rising over the Fens. When I was a child, it struck as much awe into me as it must have done to our ancient forefathers who watched it rise out of their misty horizons like some pagan god from secret waters. It always made me feel that I was witnessing something magical and primeval. This was how the world began, and life could never be the same again.

Perhaps it wasn't. Soon the gleaning days for everyone were over, and, now that men have dug and danced on the moon, it has lost a little of the mystery it once had. Or has it? As the swifts rose higher and higher, becoming almost invisible if not inaudible in the opaque sky, a half-moon rose over Framlingham Castle, and it was impossible not to feel at that moment some lunar power being exercised over the transitory lives of us lesser mortals. And if not power, then at least enough majesty and timeless beauty to be still worthy of our praise.

So, once again, 'all is safely gathered in', most of the fields are empty, the swifts will soon have left our summer skies, and another season will be over. In churches and chapels the pews and altars, chancels and choir-stalls will be decked with sprays of corn, bunches of carrots, parsnips, beetroot, apples, marrows, dahlias and chrysanthemums, and the organ will roar or wheeze into life with the opening lines of 'Come, ye thankful people, come/Raise the song of Harvest Home. . . .', depending, of course, on the prosperity or neglect experienced by the church. Whether the people will come is another matter. I doubt if I shall hear again the kind of blunt sermon I once heard many harvests ago when the flamboyant preacher chastised his enlarged congregation with the opening remark, 'Well, I must say that the church is never so popular as when it looks like a well-stocked greengrocer's shop. I don't suppose I shall see half of you again until next year, unless you want me to bury you. . . .'

What did impress me during this recent 'stay-at-home' summer was how *English* the countryside was, so much so that, in spending most of my holiday at home in the counties of East Anglia, I had the distinct feeling that I was 'abroad'. Now I know that must sound like a wild contradiction but it is the only way I can say what I mean. I just forgot that I was in England, that the rural novelties and interests were a daily part of my native land.

I suppose in these days we take overseas holidays very much for granted, and, even if we do not go on them ourselves, we become very much familiar with other landscapes, whether they are in Spain, Austria, Norway, southern France or the Seychelles. To stay at home and

An attractive village hiding in the shelter of parklands

rediscover the delights of the English landscape which still survive beyond the motorways is not unlike discovering a foreign country. Attractive villages hiding modestly in the shelter of great parklands, thatched pubs where you can eat and drink outside under a chestnut tree with the locals, old-fashioned tea-rooms with home-made cakes, silent churches and ruined castles, crowded market streets and timeless characters at crossroads—where else could they all be found in a single day?

Among the hours of summer which I shall long remember were those spent with the writer and critic Ronald Blythe, who took us for a walk through fields where Constable and Edward Fitzgerald had strolled on many occasions. A heron rose from a small lake. Larks sang above the hissing corn. Thistles grew where once farm labourers' cottages had stood. The side of a field where the oil-seed rape had been gathered had the texture of rough tweed. It was a very 'English' evening—the perfect landscape for such a meeting. As we walked back to the old house, where the artist John Nash and his wife Christine had lived, we spoke of those writers, places and memories which meant so much to us—Edwin Muir, Thomas Hardy, Edward Seago, Constable, Yeats, Jane Austen and John Nash himself. A small ginger kitten leapt about between delicate pieces of porcelain. The sun went down as slowly as the red wine we were drinking. The smell of evening drifted in through the open door. Whenever the scenes of this year's corn being cut are recalled, I shall think of the people with whom I shared a perfect season. I might even sing a verse or two of thanksgiving, when no one is listening.

21 Out of the Mists

Lincolnshire mist, like south Lincolnshire soil, is born of the sea, or it appears to be. It is different from the mist of the Cambridgeshire Fens which rises from the earth, smells of the earth and is often as heavy as earth. The mist of Lincolnshire is more phantom-like, transparent and (if you will forgive the unavoidable pun) mysterious. It has a strange quality of light about it, an opaqueness which does not erase everything from view but rather enhances it with subtle nuances. The sky becomes no more than a window which has been breathed on. Beyond the misty glass can still be seen the outlines of the familiar, but the familiar is changed. I am speaking now of early autumn mists rather than winter fogs—for I know of no county which can produce worse fogs than Lincolnshire.

A recent journey reminded me of this distinction, of this unusual effect which Lincolnshire mist has upon me, as well as upon the land. It smells of the sea and swirls like the sea. It even carries echoes of the sea and has the threat of the sea. The encounter of which I write happened one day as we were making our way home from the Wolds. My wife was driving, so I could concentrate on the exciting transformation going on around me. We were, as usual, taking the roads 'less travelled by' and were in no particular hurry. The day had been warm but sultry, with the occasional thunderstorm, and there was certainly a mist out at sea when we ventured towards the coast. That mist now crept inland, and the fields were wrapped in a grey muslin which made them look unreal and insubstantial. The harvest was over, and, as there had been less stubble-burning this year, each cornfield had the appearance of a deserted beach at sunset. The straw shone like fine sand. The dark horizon was a distant sea.

Immediately the familiar landscape took on an excitement—or, rather, I became excited about the familiar. Trees drifted in and out of my vision like a ballet of ghosts. Church spires emerged, then melted away more quickly than ice before a fire. The mist did not hover knee-deep as it does so often in the Cambridgeshire Fens; it enveloped everything from the sky down.

On the long, straight road from Revesby down to Frithville, I had the feeling that I had embarked on a journey into the unknown, a journey which could at any moment reveal some wonder or miracle.

I did not have long to wait. As we turned towards Gipsey Bridge, then crossed the River Witham towards Brothertoft, the mist thinned sufficiently for Boston Stump to appear like a faded sepia print on a Victorian sky. I have never seen the Stump (a most inappropriate nickname on this occasion) look so tall, so elegant and so ethereal. It was etched delicately but briefly on my afternoon, yet I know the memory of it will survive the mists of many years.

> I cannot explain why some moments
> equal a lifetime, why some seconds
> carve fissures quicker than waterfalls,
> but it's always happening. The mind
> dwells for a journey upon one thought
> that suddenly is shattered by a glimpse
> of someone chopping wood, a woman
> just unlocking her front door, and then . . .

And this time the moment was of that elongated tower, made more of the stuff of visions than earthly stone that was meant to last forever.

Boston qualifies for my catalogue of towns which have a definite 'spirit of place'. It may not be everyone's idea of an attractive town but it cannot be ignored, as many towns can. Like Wisbech and King's Lynn, it has the extra special something which has nothing to do with beauty. Perhaps it is the link with the sea, a taste of salt and adventure in the air.

The interesting thing about such towns which have this quality is that they often produce more than their share of

'Boston Stump appeared like a faded sepia print on a Victorian sky'

famous people, men and women who, from populations of two or three thousand, go out to change the lives of millions in all countries and for many generations.

Boston's contribution to the world has been exceptional by any standard. Apart from its associations with the early Pilgrim Fathers (who were imprisoned there in 1607 after they had been betrayed by the Dutch captain on whose ship they were sailing to escape religious persecution), the town was also the birthplace in 1516 of John Foxe, the author of what is now commonly known as Foxe's *Book of Martyrs*.

Boston can also claim John Taverner (1490–1545), the great Tudor composer of madrigals, and the poet Jean Inglelow, (1820–97), whose ballad 'High Tide on the Coast of Lincolnshire, 1571', still appears regularly in anthologies of English verse. The town's tradition of producing such creative minds continued with the birth in 1926 of one of today's outstanding poets, Elizabeth Jennings.

There are earlier literary associations with John Conington (1825–69), who, in his short life, translated much of Virgil, Aeschylus and Horace and also with Herbert Ingram, the founding editor of that still popular journal the *Illustrated London News*. Ingram, remembered in the town by his statue near the church, was drowned in 1860 while on tour in America.

The mist veiled the landscape for the rest of our journey home through Kirton, Gosberton, Pinchbeck and Bourne. It had been a day on which one would not have been surprised to see another famous figure emerging from the eerie clouds surrounding us—Hereward the Wake, that noble native of Lincolnshire who must surely be partly responsible for the proud and defiant character of all true Fenmen.

It is, however, a mistake to think of this swashbuckling warrior as nothing more than a scourge of the Normans or as an arsonist and murderer. He was undoubtedly an extremely strong and fierce leader, unwilling to compromise and excelling in war. But he also appreciated the finer things of life. He liked music, could play the harp and sang well. As a tall, handsome man he also had a reputation for being particularly charming to the ladies. Long before he became involved in the affairs of the Fenmen's struggles against the Normans, he had fought campaigns in Ireland, Cornwall and Flanders. He was renowned not only for his strength and courage but for his strategic skills and guerilla-war tactics. He always knew how to use the countryside to his advantage, as William the Conqueror found out. After his often stormy and always eventful life he retired to his estates in Lincolnshire, having made a reluctant peace with the king and regretting now that so much blood had been spilt on English soil.

And what happened then? Was he ignominiously murdered by a Frenchman with a personal vendetta, or did he die a natural death and finally enjoy a reconciliation with his wife, Torfrida, buried in Crowland Abbey?

Would he smile, or be angry, that his name is now perpetuated and better known by the young as a local radio-station or a shopping centre? Would he thank Charles Kingsley for helping to make him such a legendary figure?

There was no time for further speculation. We had reached the outskirts of that city which he had once helped to destroy, and the mist, which for me had created so many fantasies, was now barricaded out by the high buildings of the twentieth century.

Of this we can be sure, that they, like Hereward, will one day fall and the mists return. But, until then, I can relax in a comfortable haze of contentment and in the grateful satisfaction that my day has been well spent, our journey memorable.

22 A Distant Prospect

I used to think that my favourite view of Ely Cathedral was from Stuntney, when, with sudden and regal dignity, the great church rose dramatically out of the Fen with its crown of stone, causing yet again deep gasps of admiration. Perhaps it still is, but at the moment there is a strong contender. Not that I wish in any way to dismiss the impact of that view, or my desire to see it whenever possible: it is still one of the most exciting sights in the Fens; but, more and more, I find myself drawn to 'the distant prospect', to seeing the ethereal quality of that building from a few miles off. So, for the time being, my first choice would be from the banks of the Old Bedford River, looking across the Hundred Foot Washes and Nature Reserve near Welney. Better still is to see it from inside one of the hides provided for bird-watchers. Seen through the narrow aperture of a wooden hut intensifies the wonder of it, separating it from all other distractions except the birds and the nearby grazing cows. Beyond the Washlands it even appears to sail slowly into view across a green sea—a golden, mythical ship on the horizon, a voyager from another world.

I experienced the thrill of that view again the other day when I walked along the bank and shut myself in Stockdale Hide. It was a joy I had not planned or expected. It was the reward for an impulsive action. All of us have days when the work to be done just does not go well, when, for the writer especially, the pen scratches, the ink runs out, the shoulders ache with tension and the head feels more like a cannon-ball. Sometimes one has to persevere and squeeze something out of that solid lump to meet a deadline, but sometimes the frustrations override all discipline and there is only one thing to do—give in, to go back to the source, to go out into the great open spaces again to find out what it is that one is supposed to be writing about.

So with a little wise and understanding persuasion from my wife, I put the pen away and we drove off into the Fens, to escape rather than to discover. But you can't escape in the Fens. You can only return to them, be absorbed by them and feel safely at home in them. That is, I admit, a personal view and might not be shared willingly by everyone. But from the moment we got beyond Flag Fen and Benwick, I became a new man. The frustrations had dispersed like morning mist. The head now had eyes, the mind had thoughts, and I was as happy as a child going to the seaside. There again were the inspiring distances, the space, the sky, the continents of cloud and the smells of the dark soil. Cities and civilizations were left behind with all their noise and irritations. I was free. Suddenly there was a wider margin to life. Even the names of farms and fields leapt off the map and became real places, exotic, intriguing places of newly discovered land—Plantation Farm, Capalder Corner, Ranson Moor, Botany Bay, Honey Hill, Bishop's Land and Purls Bridge—poetry to the ears of anyone who responds as I do to the world they represent. Looking across the Hundred Foot Washes and South Level, there are other unlikely names to tease the imagination—Dunkirk, California, Quaker Farm and Frogs Abbey—and then, on that magical horizon, Ely Cathedral, becalmed in the stillness of an afternoon that could belong to nowhere else.

We sat in the hide and gazed out at the scene before us, more contented with what we beheld than we could have been with any landscape we knew. If you asked me to describe exactly what we saw, I doubt if I could. There were fields, reeds, willow trees, cows, water, grass and two men fishing, but such details can never convey the mystery or the compelling beauty of such a scene. There were the intangible things—light, smells, atmosphere. Perhaps it was not so much what we *saw* as what we *felt*.

I am reminded of a far bleaker day when I was out in another part of the Fens with a cameraman who was new to the landscape and had come to take pictures of it for the first time. The bemused man looked all round at the scene I had so enthusiastically chosen and said, 'What have we stopped

A distant prospect of Ely cathedral across The Hundred Foot Washes

here for? There's nothing I can film out here. The place is naked.' I understood his problem and replied, 'I know there's not much to see, but can't you *feel* it?' He rolled his eyes and through clenched teeth said, 'I can't film feelings.' Even so, he managed to evoke something of the atmosphere of that particular day and by the time we got to the Windmill on Ten Mile Bank was forgiving enough to buy me a drink.

The pen is not always much better at conveying the qualities of a day like that, or the one I write of now. You have to be there to feel the long-distant wind on your face, to hear the conspiratorial gossip of the reeds, to see the wake of gulls at the stern of a plough, to register the tremors of all that is past. You have to see the 'hidden country' and know something of its history. You look not at a day but at a thousand years. Even then you are only just beginning to scratch beneath the surface of the soil that Time has scattered, tilled and ploughed upon this land. There you might find the footprints of Hereward the Wake, the first monks of Ely or the Norman soldiers who died defending what they had so recently stolen from the Fenmen. But there were other footprints before these, and, in the silence of an autumn afternoon, there are those ghostly echoes of voices rising from the ground which can send a shiver down your spine.

We did not stay long enough to see if we would spot any of the rare birds which patient bird-watchers had seen so far that season—purple heron, blue-winged teal, red-crested pochard, red-necked phalarope, marsh-harriers, godwits, ruffs, whimbels and osprey. It was neither the time nor did we have the hours to spare. But one day, I said to myself, making yet another promise.

Yet will it ever be the same, planned and premeditated? I doubt it. One can never choose the day. One can only respond on the spur of the moment when the day calls. We shall go back, but the experience will be different. All I can hope for is that the spirit of the Fens will again be strong enough, stronger than any self-will or imposed discipline. Sometimes it pays to listen to the heart rather than the head.

As we made our way home through Manea (once earmarked by Charles I as the site of his new summer palace when the Fens were drained), through Stonea, Bedlam, Binnismoor and Creek, the setting sun cast a golden light over the fields and, yet again, turned the slender reeds to torches along the dykes. Here and there a solitary farmhand still tried to complete his day's work before the light failed, and in the distance farmhouses were visible only because of the little squares of light which shone from their windows.

Eventually we crossed the now buried Roman Causeway between Goosetree and Eldernell, pausing for a second or two to watch a heron hang-gliding to its nest at the top of a tree. Eldernell, now almost forgotten, was once an early Christian shrine and the site of a miracle-healing in 1055. A man called Robert Whyt of Whittlesey was dying. He was so weak he could not rise from his bed and could hardly speak. But one night he had a vision of the Blessed Lady of Eldernell, who promised to preserve and comfort him if he would tell the Vicar of Whittlesey to preach a sermon condemning his parishioners for 'their perpetual swearing and blasphemy, for as often as they swore they tore asunder the body of Christ, causing His wounds to bleed as freshly as they did at His crucifixion . . .'. On the following Monday Robert Whyt made signs that he wanted a clean shirt. When he had dressed, he rose from his bed and staggered to the door of his house. Then, 'with bare head and bare feet and a staff in his hands he took his pilgrimage to Our Lady of Eldernell'. He also took with him two rosaries and was followed by the vicar and some of the neighbours. 'Sparing no way he went through thick and thin in that cold frosty morning feeling no pain the space of three miles between.' When he reached Eldernell, he fell on his knees and began his prayers before the shrine of the Blessed Virgin. For fifteen minutes he was unable to speak but then cried out, 'Lady, help!' The people who had gone with him also knelt close by, each one holding a lighted candle, and all saw the tears which flowed from the eyes of the statue. At that moment Robert Whyt 'by the help of God turned again to good health and was alive'.

By the time we had reached the North Bank of the Nene, on our way to Peterborough, the sun was no more than a red smudge on the grey canvas of cloud—a painting which Turner never quite got round to finishing. If Ely Cathedral had earlier reminded me of a ship, Peterborough Cathedral emerged darkly from the horizon like the entrance to a harbour. It represented home, the voyage over.

Later still, I looked out from my window onto the deserted precincts. It was so still that I could almost hear the grass breathing under the yellow lamplight, as if it too were grateful for the night. As I stared into the shadows, my mind was full of all the images it had received that day. Even when I closed my eyes, I could see the fields, the long, empty roads, the rivers and the sky. Then the cathedral clock chimed ten, the slow, sombre notes falling like invisible snow over the grass. I turned and looked at my desk, at the remaining pages waiting for words. There was no more to be said. They would have to wait.

23 A Second Opinion

I have said in earlier chapters how necessary it is for us from time to time to see our own familiar landscape through the eyes of others, whether they are native to that landscape or not, and more and more I delight in the discovery of a paragraph, even a sentence, which gives me a new insight into scenes so easily taken for granted.

One of my most recent and surprising finds has been Hilaire Belloc, a writer I had usually associated with the south-country. Little did I realize when I picked up a second-hand copy of his *Hills and the Sea* that its pages would offer some of the best and most perceptive descriptions I had read of the Fens for a long time: 'Nowhere that I have been to in the world does the land fade into the sea so inconspicuously. . . . The dry land slips and wallows into a quiet, very shallow water, confused with a yellow thickness and brackish with the weight of inland water behind. There should be a demarcation between them, a tide-mark or limit. There is nothing. You cannot say where one begins and the other ends. One does not understand the Fens until one has seen that shore. . . .' And elsewhere he says: 'The land seems very vague, the flat line of the horizon is the only boundary and that horizon mixes into watery clouds. No countryside is so formless until one has seen the plan of it set down on a map, but on studying such a plan one understands the scheme of the Fens. . . .'

Now if every stranger approaching the Fens for the first time had sense enough to bring a large-scale map with him, he would, as Belloc did, find it easier to accept the vast, anonymous space before him. That space can, I know (from the visitors I have entertained from other parts of Britain), intimidate, frighten and over-awe. I remember some friends from South Wales stopping me half-way round a Sunday afternoon drive into the Fens, saying, 'Are you sure we shall get back? There are no landmarks, nothing . . . Duw, it's awful. I don't know how anyone could live out here.'

In Belloc's book there is an amusing account of how he was trying to find the Griffin Inn, in March, which, so a friend had told him, was beyond compare. 'If you would enjoy the Griffin you must ask your way to that town, and as you go ask also for the Griffin, for many who may not have heard of March will certainly have heard of the Griffin.' But, as Belloc discovered, 'These dykes of the Fens are accursed things: they are the separation of friends and lovers', and he lost his way. After a few unusual experiences he eventually got a lift in a horse and cart from a man who was 'going through March'. And he did just that. He drove his horse so fast that his passenger found himself several miles 'in the country beyond' before he realized that he had missed not only the town but the Griffin as well.

There are many men I know who would say, as Belloc's friend said, that you *cannot* miss the Griffin. It was the inn where I first came into contact with some of the legendary drinkers of the Fens. It was at a National Farmers' Union Dinner. I was twenty and totally bewildered in the presence of so many red-faced, robust, jovial, potato-growers, potato-merchants and other members of the farming fraternity. Little did I know then, as I shrank in a haze of cigar-smoke and giddiness, that thirty years later I would be reminded of the occasion by the chance discovery of this absorbing book of essays by a man 'from the South'.

It made me go back to books I had not read for a long time, including Charles Kingsley's novel *Hereward the Wake,* which I have vague memories of reading at school. If Hilaire Belloc was perceptive, Kingsley was persuasive—at least in his descriptions of the landscape: 'They have a beauty of their own, these great Fens, even now, when they are dyked and drained, tilled and fenced—a beauty of the sea, of boundless expanse and freedom. . . . That vastness still gives such cloudlands, such sunrises, such sunsets, as can be seen nowhere else within these isles. . . .'

Whether all Fenmen would agree with Kingsley's assessment of their character is another matter:

> The lowlander is not for the most part picturesque or poetical. He finds out soon enough for his weal and bane that he is stronger than Nature, and right tyrannously and irreverently he lords it over her, clearing, delving, building without fear or shame. He knows no natural force greater than himself, save an occasional thunderstorm, and against that, as he grows more cunning, he insures his crops. Why should he reverence Nature? He has little or nothing around him to refine or uplift his soul; and unless he meet with a religion and with a civilization which can deliver him, he may sink into that dull brutality which is too common amongst the lowest classes of the English lowlands, and remain for generations gifted with the strength and industry of the ox, and with the courage of the lion, but alas, with the intellect of the former and the self-restraint of the latter. . . .

Ox, lion or tiger, it is clear that the character of Fenland people has frequently caused commentators to refer to our strength, endurance, stubbornness, cunning and aggression rather than our intelligence or refinement of spirit. But when one considers what vicissitudes, tragedies and conflicts with the elements the Fenman has had to contend, it is not surprising that he has developed a certain toughness and defiance in his character. As we shall see from the following chapter, the odds have often been against him, and he has needed to be a fighter if only to protect his land from his great enemy—water.

More recently I have been looking again at the writings of Dorothy L. Sayers, who spent her childhood in the Fens and certainly used the landscape in her writings, most notably in *The Nine Tailors*. How many winter visitors must have shared Lord Peter Wimsey's feelings after his car crash at Frog's Bridge in the snow: 'Next time I accept hospitality in the Fen-country, I'll take care that it's at midsummer.'

Equally, how many of us have not shared that desolate view where 'road and dyke marched on side by side into an eternity of winter'? It was a scene which Miss Sayers saw very often as a young girl when her father was Rector of Bluntisham-cum-Earith. She saw also how the nearby

Washlands were frequently flooded to protect the farmlands, and heard from the local people much of the Fenland history which she was to use later in her novels. As well as a good eye for landscape, she had a good ear for local dialogue, and the conversations in *Nine Tailors* ring true with a freshness that you could hear in those villages today.

It is impossible to mention all the novels which have the Fens as their setting, or indeed to refer to the many poems which have the Fens as their subject. There is, I believe, a literature of the Fens, and, as well as the many topographical and academic books, there is a growing body of work which reflects the life of the Fens. I think especially of books like Sybil Marshall's *Fenland Chronicle*, W. H. Barrett's *Tales from the Fens* and the many personal reminiscences which have appeared, often in modest publications but nevertheless preserving the experience of people who have all, in their own way, added to our history. One of the finest and most evocative of recent novels must be *Waterland* by Graham Swift.

Of the poetry to come out of the Fens, it is inevitable, I suppose, after a lifetime's interest in the man, that I should turn to John Clare. Although he was not a Fenman, coming as he did from that gentle northern corner of Northamptonshire, he regularly made excursions into the lowlands or took, as it were from a distance, a bird's eye view of the great Fens spread out before him to the east. For him they were 'like a richly coloured map', where the arch of light 'Stretches for days its cloudless sky' and where the great clouds on the horizon became his only mountains. But he wrote not only of the landscape in summer. He was often better describing the winter scene:

So moping flat and low our valleys lie
So dull and muggy is our winter sky
Drizzling from day to day with threats of rain
And when that falls still threatening on again;
From one wet week so great an ocean flows
That every village to an island grows
And every road for even weeks to come
Is stopt and none but horsemen go from home.

Clare's publishers and friends could not understand how he ever found inspiration in such a dull landscape. Writing in the *London Magazine*, in November 1821, John Taylor said: 'A flatter country than the immediate neighbourhood can scarcely be imagined', and Octavius Gilchrist, writing in the same magazine a year earlier, made the point even more strongly: 'Fancy, surely, can scarcely suggest scenery less fitted for the excitement of picturesque and vivid description, than the dank copses and sedgy margin of the Fens.' Clare himself admitted in a letter to Edward Drury that, 'The Fens are not a literary part of England', and yet he has brought more literary pilgrims to the area than most and has contributed a large portion to the literature we have. The John Clare Society now has three hundred members, many of them from overseas, and hardly a week passes without someone visiting the villages of Helpston and Northborough from which he gained so much inspiration.

With winter not too far away, I shall soon begin to share Clare's delight in that season if only because it allows one a little more reading time. For Clare it was not only more reading time but also a rest from those long, hard days of working in the fields:

'Tis winter and I love to read indoors
When the moon hangs her crescent up on high
While on the window shutters the wind roars
And storms like furies pass remorseless by.
How pleasant on a feather-bed to lie
Or, sitting by the fire, in fancy soar
With Dante, or with Milton to regions high
Or read fresh volumes we've not seen before. . . .

Fresh volumes! Ah, there's a thought to warm the heart! All those volumes bought greedily from second-hand bookshops during the summer months, waiting for the moment when they will be opened in front of a log fire some winter afternoon when there is nothing more rewarding than to share in another man's thoughts.

Knowing that others have looked at my landscape in their own way, either to praise or to condemn, makes me use my own eyes more searchingly, more keenly and more hopefully to see those beauties or mysteries still waiting to be revealed. For I look now not with my eyes only but with the appreciation and eyes of others who have looked at this land for centuries. Eyes can be ageless.

24 The Epic Drama of '47

In trying to establish the character of Fen people, we are forced again to consider their many struggles with the elements during the last few centuries. No landscape is more exposed to fierce winds, long winters, dry summers, drought, damp or flooding—a mixture of extremes far more dramatic than the 'occasional thunderstorm' referred to by Charles Kingsley.

A lifetime spent on the land, season by season, whether ploughing, hoeing sugar-beet, celery-lifting or harvesting, inevitably influences a man's character. As I said at the beginning of this book, the soil itself can condition a man's life more than we realize, and the Fens appear to have a particular power over the events of men.

By far the greatest conflict they have had with nature has been with water. It has bred in every Fenman a hostility, caution, fear and, at times, bitterness. It has also produced an heroic defiance and a determination not to be beaten by nature, an attitude which led Kingsley to say that the lowlander 'knows no natural force greater than himself' and has little 'reverence for Nature'.

Nowhere in recent Fenland history has this been more courageously expressed than in the now famous story of the floods of 1947. There had been many episodes of serious flooding for as long as Man could remember. The low-lying nature of the land, the high-flowing rivers, the vulnerability of sea-walls, and the problems of getting surplus water out into the Wash, had too often made the threat a reality. But 1947 was an epic on the heroic scale which will never be forgotten.

No one could have imagined during the early March days of that year that such drama and tragedy would be witnessed by the end of the month. It is true that men whose job it was to watch the water-levels were worried by a number of factors. There had been a long winter with recent heavy falls of snow. Severe frosts had cracked the soil of the flood-banks, and a sudden thaw in the uplands could create an enormous weight of water for the Fenland rivers to hold. Even so, all the modern drainage equipment was expected to cope—if only the sea tides did not make it impossible to use Denver Sluice and if the normally notorious winds of March remained docile.

As if nature intended to prove her superiority over helpless mortals, she contrived to demonstrate her power by arranging for all three elements to come together. In military terms, it was like having the full might of the Army, Navy and Air Force in a combined attack on one battle zone. The snows melted quickly, pouring millions of gallons of water each hour into the rivers. High tides meant that Denver Sluice could not be operated fully, thereby preventing upland water from reaching the Wash. And the March winds, far from being docile, reached speeds of up to one hundred miles an hour.

It was manifestly clear to those who watched that all the flood-protection schemes were about to be severely tested. The alert went out as the water continued to rise. 'Strengthen the banks! Bring up extra supplies of gault and sand! Start sandbagging, and prepare for the worst!' The Hundred Foot Washes could only take so much. The Great Ouse and its tributaries would soon overflow if these conditions prevailed. It might even be necessary to evacuate those people living in the most threatened areas. And this was so.

By 13 March the roads between Earith and Welney were under water and almost impassable. Floods were rising everywhere in the Fens at a frightening rate. It soon became apparent that there was no way in which the problem could be isolated to just one district. This was an all-out attack.

The water in the Ouse reached bank level—which was between fifteen and twenty feet above the level of the surrounding land. The wind kept up its relentless battering, bringing down trees and telegraph poles, blocking roads which were a vital source of communication.

'No one could have imagined that such a drama would be witnessed'

In Ely people began to evacuate their homes, or to raise their furniture on piles of bricks to clear the water now creeping into their houses. In some streets it was already a foot deep. Soon the surrounding villages stood helplessly marooned. The road through Chittering was closed. The railway station at Littleport was flooded, trains were stopped.

By Sunday evening, 16 March, news came through that the River Lark, beyond Prickwillow, was about to burst its banks. Villagers in Burnt Fen were advised by the police to leave their homes and accept the safety offered at Mildenhall Air Base.

Now every pair of hands was employed in raising the level of the banks with more gault and more sandbags. But it was an uneven match. The wind, still at hurricane force, was whipping up twenty-foot waves, making it difficult for the workmen to stand up. More roads became impassable, and the problem of getting emergency supplies to the men became even more serious.

Soldiers stationed in the area were detailed to help. So too were German prisoners of war who had still not been repatriated by the Government. The Fen landscape resembled even more a muddy battlefield, with Army vehicles, amphibious tanks, lighting equipment and officers working alongside the drainage engineers.

By Monday morning the grey daylight revealed how great the task was for everyone. Vast areas of land were now submerged. And still the water poured down from Bedfordshire and Northamptonshire. Within hours there were two further major breaches of the Ouse, at Over and at Little Thetford. The villages of Willingham and Over were quickly flooded and as the water gushed down to Earith and the Old West River, more than two thousand acres of rich farmland were drowned. One of the ironies of the disaster was that the rivers could not even be used for transporting supplies. The water-level of the disaster was now so high that barges could not pass under the bridges.

Despite all the odds against them, the men fought on. A one-hundred-foot-wide break had now developed in the Ouse, and the Old West was on the point of bursting. By midday the battle was lost. Water poured over the banks, drowning a further three thousand acres at Hillrow Fen. There was nothing to do now but retreat. The gangs of men were called from their impossible tasks, and every kind of vehicle that was available was used in getting people, stock and possessions away from the areas of devastation.

By nightfall the scene was one of total desolation. An enormous lake of brown water now covered the earth, and only a few isolated roof-tops showed where deserted houses stood. On distant roads could still be seen the grey, straggling processions of homeless families, moving slowly and shocked, like refugees, pushing their carts and prams loaded with whatever they had managed to save.

Conditions worsened by Wednesday morning. Haddenham Fen was flooded to a depth of twelve feet; a ninety-foot-wide gap now split the bank of the River Wissey, and Hilgay Fen was under water within minutes. There was not a single portion of the Fen country remaining unthreatened. Every river had reached breaking point—the Lark, the Little Ouse, the Cam and the Nene. To co-ordinate the rescue work a military headquarters was established in the preparatory department of Ely High School, and the campaign was nicknamed 'Operation Noah's Ark'. Noah could not have been in greater need of help.

It was inevitable that, coming so soon after the Second World War, there should have been these military comparisons. The British people were, after all, facing a similar crisis, a battle for survival. The same war-time spirit prevailed. People took in strangers, made pots of tea and provided blankets. Organizations such as the Women's Institute, the Salvation Army, the Red Cross and the WVS ran canteens, cooked meals and ferried the elderly to safety. In one make-shift canteen (at the Peacock Inn, Ely), an average of three thousand sandwiches a day were made and taken out to the men working on the banks or given to the homeless, all at a time when food was still scarce.

Seven days after the troubles had first started, the water continued pouring down into the Fens, and men were rushed to various stretches of the rivers where there was any hope of saving the banks. Thousands of sandbags were filled to erect a mile-long barrier between Ferry Inn and Southery, where the water was rising six inches an hour.

But the water could only be held back for so long. Stemmed in one place, it broke out in another. On Saturday 22 March the dam in the culvert near Southery collapsed under the weight of water, and all the efforts of the work-gangs were contemptuously brushed aside. It had been hoped that the rich Fens of Southery and Feltwell would be saved. Other areas had been allowed to flood in order to protect them. Now the violence of the released water ripped open the main road and rushed in a ninety-foot-wide torrent across the fields. The men who had worked round the clock for several days could only turn wearily away and surrender. The force of water was so great that it tore a solid, double-fronted house in half. The owner's belongings, which had been stored upstairs for safety, were swept away like matchsticks—easy chairs, a settee, tables and cupboards, all of little consequence in the path of the flood.

And so the great epic continued until the end of the month. Gradually the waters began to subside and the men were able to resume repair work to the river banks. But nothing could save the thirty thousand acres around them that were still under water.

People returned to their homes, but the houses were uninhabitable. One man was able to row a boat through the walls of his bungalow, and even those houses which had withstood the floods now had windows blown out by the gales or were occupied by hundreds of rats. Most garden sheds and greenhouses had been smashed to the ground, and scores of domestic animals had perished. It was a sight people knew they would never forget, an episode they would talk about to their grandchildren.

A similar battle had been fought in the northern Fens between Thorney and Crowland. Hugh Cave remembers it well. He and his men were called out several times to do emergency repair work on the drains:

'The river bank had already broken at Crowland, and on the Saturday afternoon we were asked to put in a dam on the French Drove drain to prevent the water flooding farmland. We were called out again on Sunday afternoon and worked right through until two o'clock on Monday morning. But it was clear that the amount of water coming into the area was not going to be contained. We put a steel dam in at Thorney Bridge in an effort to stop the floods getting south of the Thorney River, but the water broke through and reached Wryde Corner before we knew what had happened. I don't know where we would have been without all the hard work which was done by the German prisoners of war from the Thorney Camp. They did a magnificent job, and I don't think I've ever seen men work harder. It was, if I remember correctly, Easter weekend, but there was no chance of celebrating Easter or having a few days off. On Good Friday a brick culvert collapsed and we had to replace it with a three-foot concrete tube. The men worked all through the weekend in order to get it finished. Fortunately we were able to divert a lot of the floodwater into the River Nene, so conditions were not as bad as they might have been.'

But it was a different story for the people of Crowland. As early as the Tuesday of that week the town crier had been out in the streets calling for volunteers to help repair the bursting banks of the River Welland. Despite their efforts the bank burst at midday on the following Friday, and the Fens between Newborough and Eye were flooded.

As water poured into the fields, sixteen amphibious Buffalo tanks were brought in by the Army in an attempt to close the breach in the river. But, as the rains continued into April, even these heavy monsters were swept away. Twenty thousand acres were inundated, and the floodwater created a lake of twenty square miles.

In all, sixty thousand acres of rich farmland were under water that spring, and it was thought that some of the land would never be used for arable crops again. But the Fenmen had reclaimed the land from the waters before and they would do so this time. Their spirit was not broken. They would defy the old aggressor and make those fields once more the most productive in England.

And so it was. The resilience, stubbonness, pride, courage and total unwillingness to be beaten engraved into Fenmen's hearts and history an epic which will stand for all time as a marvellous example of their character.

Although this chapter has concentrated on the floods of 1947, it does not wish to ignore the disasters which have occurred since. In January 1953 the whole of East Anglia was threatened again by one of the most disastrous sea-floods in living memory. The combination of high winds and rising tides soon meant that the water-level was up to eight feet above normal before anyone could do much about it. Sea-walls were brushed aside by gigantic waves, river-banks burst and thousands of acres of good farmland were soon under water. This time, because most of that water was salt, it took five years for the land to recover.

Similarly, in January 1978 flooding was aggravated by gale-force winds which stripped houses of their roofs, tore down barns and uprooted trees, creating a scene of devastation to equal those of 1947, and many before.

Wisbech was, once again, victim of these twin terrors. A fierce tidal surge in the Wash caused the Nene to burst its banks even before the tide reached its peak, and a fifth of the town was under water within an hour. As before, people piled sandbags at their doors and moved all their furniture upstairs. Cars were swept away like Dinky toys, animals perished before they could be reached, and hospital patients had to be evacuated to safer wards in Peterborough and Norwich. And, as always, when the drama was over, there were the pathetic scenes of clearing up: ruined carpets stacked outside waiting for the refuse-lorries, interior decorations beyond repair, the smell of damp which lasted for months, the expression of despair, defeat, anger, helplessness, and then the resolution to start again.

No man-written drama has ever produced a greater villain or so many heroes. And we do not even know whether the last act has been played out or not. It is hardly likely when we remember what has already been recorded in our history.

25 Tales from the George and Dragon

When I had finished my brief period of National Service in 1949—brief because after the strenuous initial training I was, as one of our neighbours gleefully used to say, 'unmedically fit'—I returned home not knowing what to do with myself. I had never felt fitter in all my life and was not at all worried about being medically discharged. Some of my friends in the same squadron were similarly dismissed because they had suffered with cramp or stammered.

Having started work in a solicitor's office when I left school, I knew from my recent experience of the great wide world that law was not the career I wished to follow, nor one for which I was particularly well suited. It was time to make a new start to life. I was all of twenty.

Fortunately I discovered that a family of farmers and potato-merchants in Whittlesey needed an addition to its small office staff—someone who could do shorthand and typing, answer the telephone, *and* preferably male. The prevailing language in the office during the most active hours of the day, I believe, had something to do with this decision.

As I was the only applicant, the job was mine. I started nervously, hardly knowing the difference between a King Edward potato and a cricket ball. But for the next six years I had one of the most leisurely, comfortable and happy periods of employment I have ever had working for someone else. (Working for oneself is a different matter.) During the less active hours of the day I made myself look industrious by writing some of my early poems.

It was at the firm of L. C. Giddens Ltd., that I met Steve Wesley and began to learn a little more of life in the Fens. Steve was the buyer-salesman and knew most of the

'If you'd done a good day's work there was nothing anyone could grumble about'

farmers in the area. He was born at Stretham, had spent much of his childhood in that area and the Old West River and was enthusiastic about the landscape which I was now beginning to recognize as something special.

Through my new job I became more aware of the pattern of the year, in agricultural terms. The work was seasonal, the crops varied, the conversation in the office was inevitably about some problem on the land, some farm foreman or character who had earned a reputation for himself. If I had known what I know now, I would have listened more carefully to those stories of thirty-five years ago, for many of those men are gone and the world of farming has changed forever.

So it was timely that I recently met up again with Steve, who is now retired and spends a large portion of his leisure time on gardening and wood-turning. But he still has his finger on the pulse of Fenland life and knows just where to go to meet a few old Fen tigers. His friend and ex-colleague Gary McCluskey, who is now the landlord of the George and Dragon in Littleport, willingly agreed to arrange a morning when several of his customers would 'drop in for an extra pint'.

We left Whittlesey along the familiar route through Coates, Goosetree and March and drove towards Welney. For mile after mile Steve was able to refer to the names of farms and fields, all from personal association, and I said, 'You know this landscape as well as your own backyard, don't you!'

'You'd have a job to lose me out here, that's for sure. My mother was born in Welney, and I should think I've been in most of the old houses hereabouts, or know their history.'

'How much have the Fens changed in your lifetime?'

'Beyond recognition . . . Farms are much larger, for one thing, and the younger generations of farmers are certainly a different breed from their fathers . . . I can remember a time when a Fenman's word was his bond. You can't always say that now. But I suppose that's the same everywhere. Money's the all-important factor now.'

It was a pleasure to be driving slowly through the Fens on such a morning and sharing the memories of so many happy days. In the distance we could see Ely Cathedral.

'What a marvellous building that is,' said Steve, 'and aren't we lucky still to have so much wonderful cathedral music! I've spent many hours in there and enjoyed every minute.'

Our arrival at the pub had hardly been kept a secret, and, apart from having a brass band to meet us, everyone else in Littleport seemed to know we were coming. Although it was only just after opening-time, the bar was already busy. The landlord gave us a wink, and several of the men waited for me to produce a tape-recorder or a notebook, or to say something encouraging. As I never use a tape-recorder and keep my small notebook inconspicuous for as long as possible, I was left with uttering something thought-provoking like, 'Morning. Are we going to get some rain at last?'

Fortunately the rattle of dominoes and the quiet thud of darts began to ease the tension, and the bar-room conversation began to settle down to normal. I was still trying to remember some of the names of the men I had been introduced to when one of them directed his first words to me.

'You wouldn't get an atmosphere like this in one of them posh pubs with plushy carpets, would you?'

'You want to watch 'im,' said another, quickly getting into the act. ' 'E's sharper than a packet of needles. Biggest rogue in Littleport.'

More customers arrived until there were about twenty pushing their way to the bar, all trying unsuccessfully to conceal their curiosity at this 'writer bloke' who had come to pick their brains.

Although they were now nearly all Littleport men, they came originally from Feltwell, Burnt Fen, Shippea Hill and Prickwillow and knew that corner of the Fens as well as anyone can. Arthur Turner, who had just celebrated his eighty-second birthday, had worked for only two masters in fifty-two years. 'I've done every job there is on the land. My father was a horse-keeper before me, and what he didn't know wasn't worth knowing.'

Soon there were so many conversations going on around me that I knew that I would have to single out just two or three if I was going to get any answers to my questions. Inevitably, to begin with, the stories were humorous, often bawdy and always well told. The topics ranged from castration to cricket, from the merits of whisky to the harmful effects of drinking too much tap-water, from the shambles of the Common Market to the achievements or disasters of Mrs Thatcher.

I decided that two of the men who clearly had something interesting to tell me were Arthur Turner and George Ellingham, who was also retired and living alone in Littleport—though his working days had been mostly in the Feltwell area. George could remember well the drama of the 1947 floods when the Little Ouse burst its banks and so much of the land around him was under water.

'It wasn't only the water coming off the banks. It seemed to be coming up from underneath the ground as well. I could see my garden rising up and down like that, pumping like a man's heart. That were bloody frightening, I can tell you. And then the end of my house blew out. Was just washed away.'

George knew more than he was prepared to tell about the old days of poaching, wildfowling and fishing. He had learnt most of his skills from his father but also picked up a few from the gipsies.

'My father could set a trap for a hare in a forty-acre field and get him within two nights. But sometimes I was able to teach him a thing or two, and he didn't like that. When I were a boy, there were forty-four miles of dykes on 750 acres of land. You could have a lot of fun then . . . You mentioned eels. I've caught more eels in a week than most of this lot have seen in a lifetime. I got eighty on one Sunday morning alone. I once caught an eel that weighed six pounds two ounces. It took me and my landlady two days to eat it. We had it for breakfast, dinner and tea. That were beautiful. My wife died when she was thirty-one. You should never skin an eel. It spoils 'em. You should stew them with their skins on, with onions and thyme. Then they're lovely.'

'Did you ever go lark-snaring?'

'That I did. Hundreds of times. We'd have a net twenty-five foot long and fourteen foot wide, and we'd trannel that over a clover field and get scores of the critters. Larks like clover.'

'But you had to make sure', said Arthur, 'that you didn't get any bunting-larks in the net cus that's got a tooth.'

'That's right. If you got a bunting-lark in your net, he could bite his way through that like a pair of pliers.'

I discovered that there was a difference between snaring—'hingling'—and netting—'trannelling'. George used to trannel with nets. I also heard how the larks were prepared for London and found myself wincing at the thought of it.

'I've seen our kitchen table covered,' said George. 'My mother would have them all laid out neat like, with their breasts cut open ready. That's all the restaurants wanted them for—their breasts. Larks' breasts were beautiful if you got enough of 'em.'

'How much did you get for them?'

'Three-apence a dozen.'

'Didn't you ever feel that it was cruel?'

'Why should I? Not half as cruel as the poor little buggers today that are scorched to death with weed-killers or stubble-burning. At least we killed 'em outright by breaking their necks. We had to live. You took from the land what you could.'

The conversation turned to celery-growing, and Arthur told me how he had been the fastest celery-tyer in Cambridgeshire for thirty-six years when he worked at Prickwillow.

'There was no one quicker, especially for tying with rye-straw at the leaf-end and string at the root. . . . That was the way some of our customers liked it. A dozen sticks to a bundle, and each bundle tied top with rye-straw, bottom with string. I could do 250 bundles like that in a day, all with my left hand cus I didn't have all my fingers on the right, as you can see. It was big celery too. It was always mounded up three times for natural bleaching while that was growing, and a bundle could weigh six stone or more. That took a lot of chucking into the lorries. We had to do our own digging and loading. During the Second World War I had two diggers working for me, and I could tie over fourteen hundred bundles a day, just tying with string, mind you!'

'You said earlier that you had only worked for two masters in fifty-two years. They must have been good farmers to work for.'

'I can't grumble. If you'd done a good day's work to the best of your ability, there was nothing anyone could grumble about. I was lucky though. Not all the farmers were good bosses. Some were that mean they wouldn't even give you a "good-morning". But I'll say this about them, they were allus there at half past five in the morning to make sure you were on time.'

'Would you have liked to have done anything else in your life?'

'Not really. I tried to volunteer for the Army once, just to get out of the slub.'

'What's that?'

'Slub? It's that old black Fen soil when it's wet and clarty and you sink in up to your knees. I were fed up with that. But the Army wouldn't have me. I was crippled—my trigger-finger was missing.'

'You mean you were "unmedically fit",' I said, remembering what had been said about me. 'And now that you are eighty-two, what do you do with yourself?'

'Cook my meals, keep the place tidy, make horse-radish and mint sauce, toddle down here sometimes to have a chat.'

'Do you make strong horse-radish?'

'That'll burn the hairs off your chest if you're not careful. I don't put no cream or mayonnaise in mine. It's all good pure horse-radish. Would you like some? They say that's good for your love-life.'

I promised I would call at his house before we left for home. George returned with another drink and we began to talk about pheasants—how to shoot them and how to cook them.

'A pheasant should hang for five weeks, until its tail-feathers drop out. Then that's ready for eating. It smells a bit when you first start cooking it. But that passes after an hour, and when it's done it tastes lovely.'

The rain, which I had so idly forecast at the beginning of these conversations, arrived. Within minutes a thunderstorm crashed away outside, and the pub lights went out for a moment. The noise of the thunder increased the noise of the bar. Voices grew louder and the laughter more boisterous. The jokes took on tones of greater sexuality in which the prowess of one or two of the customers became a feature.

While all this was going on, the landlord quietly produced two substantial ploughman's lunches for his guests, and we took the opportunity to eavesdrop on other conversations while we ate. When I had finished my lunch, I asked George why he liked living in the Fens.

'Well, they leave you alone, don't they! You can be independent out here and nobody bothers you. It's always been the same. There's a law for the English, and there's a law for Fenmen—if you see what I mean.'

'Do you know anyone locally who is a descendant of the Littleport rioters?'

'That's hardly likely is it? They were all sent to Botany Bay, except them that was hanged.'

At this point Arthur pulled a small brown jar of pills from his pocket. 'What are they for?' I asked.

'Angina! She's thirty-five years younger'n what I am.'

'Tell 'im that dirty poem what you know, Arthur,' said George. 'You know, the one what has nineteen verses.'

'I daresn't'

But he did, stopping every other verse to ask if he 'was going too far'.

The clock hands crept dangerously near to closing-time. There were just too many stories to hear in one day, too many interesting people to meet all at once. But it had been a good morning, and I have a feeling that Steve had not found the hours too tiresome. He'd had the company of men I did not even get round to speaking to and looked equally disappointed when it was time to go.

As I drove away from Littleport, with two jars of horse-radish and two jars of mint sauce, I knew that I had also discovered a very friendly gathering-place for old Fen tigers who still kept alive the spirit of the Fens.

'Now that you've broken the ice,' said Steve, 'you'll be able to go back on your own one day and really get them going.'

But it won't be the same. In meeting up with Steve again, I had been able to put the clock back thirty years and re-live some of my own memories. For the rest of my day, even though I had tasks very far removed from the interests of the George and Dragon, I could still hear that Babel of voices, the click and rattle of dominoes, and the ghostly notes of a thousand songless larks who were sent to London for someone else's greedy pleasure.

Could I ever do more than scratch the surface of this landscape and its extraordinary people? Not if I lived for another fifty years.

26 Not Only Grantchester

It remains true, no doubt, that generally speaking one of the most well-known poets of the First World War is still Rupert Brooke (though by no means the most widely read these days), and one of his best-known and most often quoted poems must be 'The Old Vicarage, Grantchester'. Even people who claim to be totally ignorant about English verse can trot out 'Oh, yet/Stands the church clock at ten to three?/And is there honey still for tea?'

Because of that poem, written in a Berlin café in 1912, Grantchester has become an essential place of pilgrimage for thousands of visitors each year who half expect to see the young poet still taking afternoon tea in the orchard. Grantchester comes off pretty well in the poem, but there are many villages which do not. The girls of Ditton, we are told, 'are mean and dirty', and the people of Shelford 'Have twisted lips and twisted hearts', while Coton is 'full of nameless crimes/And things are done you'd not believe/At Madingley on Christmas Eve'. We are also informed that, 'At Over they fling oaths at one/And worse than oaths at Trumpington.' And as for the reputation of immorality in St Ives, or the men of Royston who 'Are black and fierce and strange of mouth. . . .'—well, the heart trembles at the thought of living in such a peculiar county after reading such descriptions.

So how true were those tongue-in-cheek accusations, I wondered. Fortunately I have been visiting some of them recently and can happily report that life now seems quite normal, as normal as anywhere can be these days. I found the people of Royston extremely warm, courteous and friendly when I was invited to give a talk there, while the natives of Coton turned out to be as harmless and innocent as villagers elsewhere. Madingley is such a beautiful village that one cannot imagine anything unseemly happening there, especially on Christmas Eve.

I was in Madingley again on a lovely golden autumn day and thought how timeless and peaceful it still was. There are few churches in the region which can offer such a delightful prospect as you step out of the porch. On that early November day the silver birch trees were dazzlingly bright with colour, and the sky was reflected in the small lake nearby. To my left, beyond a further display of autumn trees, stood Madingley Hall, stately, dignified and glowing graciously with its royal connections. Built in 1543, it once offered shelter to Charles I and, in 1861, was used by the then Prince of Wales when he was an undergraduate at Cambridge. The Hall now belongs to the University and one could not want a more serene setting for a place of learning.

I spent that afternoon sauntering round several neighbouring villages before making my way home to the Fens and found Bourn almost as appealing as Madingley, with several houses which made me covetous. This area of our country is so different from the usual fenland scenes I write about that I have to admit to being willingly seduced by the charm of its gently undulating fields and the greater abundance of its trees. Comberton, Toft and Barton were new to me, and each had an interest worth stopping for, even though my time was limited and the afternoon light was beginning to fade.

One place which is difficult to pass without pausing in for a few moments is the American War Cemetery, a silent, noble but shattering reminder of those men who died in the Second World War. The crescent rows of white crosses mark the graves of 3,811 military dead, and the roll-call on 'The Wall of the Missing' records the names of 5,125 servicemen whose graves are unknown. It is always a moving experience to stand there on that beautiful slope of English soil and to be made aware of that generation who, like Rupert Brooke's generation, made the great sacrifice. From the steps of the Memorial Chapel I could see Ely Cathedral again, clear in the autumn sunlight, and as the fallen leaves scurried quietly along the path, the pity and the gratitude were overwhelming.

The country roads I travelled that day were mercifully quiet, allowing time for thought. Frequently I stopped the car and walked the headlands of a field or made my solitary way up to a village church to learn a little more of the county's history. But a November afternoon is brief, and I had to restrict myself to moments rather than hours, promising myself that I would be back one day when time was more generous.

Eventually I had to turn homewards, passing Caxton Gibbet on my way to join the noisy flow of traffic on the A1. There had been no plan to my unexpected afternoon. I had been to Cambridge for the morning and simply 'took the road less travelled by' on my return, which made all the difference. I had no map, I just followed my nose and the whims of signposts I had never followed before. In doing so I discovered corners of the county which made my impulsive action very worthwhile. 'Adventure', wrote H. M. Tomlinson, 'is never anywhere unless we make it', and one of the many virtues of Cambridgeshire is that it can always provide adventure because it is so varied and so full of interest.

Ahead of me the late sun burned itself out on the horizon, its glowing embers scattered along the rim of the world as if the whole earth had been scorched by its fire. Even when the sun itself had disappeared, the sky throbbed like a wound until the grey clouds from the north extinguished the last spark of day. Then it began to rain and there was only one place where I wanted to be—home.

And what of Grantchester? Yes, it deserves its praise. And who can argue with Rupert Brooke when he says that Cambridgeshire of all England is 'The Shire for Men who Understand'? Who would not, when lonely in some foreign land, long to be back in any lovely English village rich with history and tradition and, at a certain time of the afternoon, have 'honey still for tea'?

A writer who would have got 'under the skin' of the Fens and brought her own poetic perception to an accurate understanding of this landscape is the much-neglected Margiad Evans, who was born in 1909 and died in 1958, before her talent was widely recognized. Poet, novelist and—some would say—nature-mystic, she had an originality of mind reminiscent of Emily Dickinson and Henry David Thoreau.

Like Thoreau, who needed a wide margin to life, Margiad Evans loved solitude and 'the edgeless hours' of a summer's day. Phrase after phrase she is able to make us *feel* and *see* as if for the first time: 'Twilight lasted and lasted until it wore itself out on the wall. . . .' 'The trees appeared to have put on flesh; their silence was softer than in frost time. . . .' 'The windows look as if they have been dipped in black oil. . . .' 'The wind is a tooth in the breast. . . .' 'I am so cold. I crouch here like a stone over a grave and the room grows empty.'

Her autobiography is a wonderful book to live with, because it holds, like a fly in amber, a whole world of seasons, sensations, ideas and reflections. Whether she is writing of the 'great starless silences' or 'The snow stretching its paws towards the back door', or 'the brown slight birds [who] throw themselves over the hedgerows like a handful of pebbles', she is expanding our own awareness of a universe for which few of us can ever find words to express our wonder and gratitude. She always longed, she said, 'to put on record my joy in *life* and *earth*'. There was for her 'hardly a day or a night without some sharp, almost painful moment of perception. There was no empty time, no era when my senses did not fly to me with wonders.'

At about the same time that Margiad Evans was writing of her joy in solitude and the need for long periods of silence, Max Picard wrote: 'Silence has been banished from the world. . . . Without silence we cannot learn, for the silent power of the landscape needs the silence in the human face if it is to exert its influence.'

What, then, would both these writers say of the world today, where silence has been not only banished but made irretrievable by the barrier of noise we have built around us?

Silence is not negative but a positive, complete world in itself, creating the right atmosphere in which we can stand and listen to what the stillness has to say. Silence is, or used to be, a reality. Thoreau wished 'to hear the silence of the night, for silence is something positive to be heard'. For

Christina Rossetti silence was 'more musical than any song'. And Wordsworth wrote enthusiastically of 'the silence of the starry sky'.

Not any more he wouldn't. Silence is outlawed, day and night, and one now has to search longer and deeper for any fugitive silence which may be left. I knew a time when it was necessary only to go beyond the boundaries of my town to enjoy stillness and silence. It is no longer so. Days when I could sit by a stream for a couple of hours without the eardrums being battered by alien sounds are becoming increasingly rare if not already a memory.

I suppose it was inevitable that city life should surrender to noise; noise to cover up noise; noise to make you forget noise—as if that were possible. Now it is impossible to shop, eat or drink without an aural backcloth of jungle drum-beats and distressed screams rising from the torture racks in hell. Today we can have 'music' wherever we go, from the dentist's chair to the crematorium, from the airliner seat to the operating table. Music (and I use the word in a very liberal sense) is now so mobile that it can intrude anywhere—on mountain tops, on secluded beaches and, yes, even in the heart of the Fens, either from milk-floats, tractors, barns or hayricks. Try going to a *quiet* restaurant or a pub to enjoy an evening's conversation with a friend. By the time you are half-way through the main course, you realize that you are shouting at each other, and everyone else is shouting too. Then why not stay at home? Shut yourself into your own silent world and enjoy the peace you want there? One can, it's true. But it is not always a guarantee. Music today can be so over-amplified that a Rock Festival two miles away can batter down the walls of one's own sitting-room. What a few hundred people want can be imposed on the whole population of a city. And if it is not the radio, then it is the aircraft overhead, hell-bent on destroying any stillness one has managed to find in the country. I do appreciate all the arguments for the planes being there. I understand the meaning of 'Defence' and the need to protect ourselves. But I do wish they would stop following me around.

I am reminded of an early autumn afternoon last year when, from all the portents of the Meteorological Office and our horoscopes, my wife and I should have had a perfect day. Could anything be more restful or restoring on such a day than a picnic in a country park? The sun still had sufficient strength to warm every bone and muscle of the spine, the trees had not yet begun to shed their yellowing leaves, and the children had all gone back to school. The only threat to our peace seemed to be a couple of inquisitive, but not angry, wasps. Perfect you might think. But we had only just unpacked the picnic basket when the most ear-splitting sound approached from beyond the sheltering bushes, and a low-flying, menacing fighter skimmed so low over the tree-tops that the trees had to duck. As we watched the anonymous plane fly over, we charitably assumed that some poor pilot had lost either his way or his lunch and wished to share ours. But it was not so. He flew over and roared his way to the other side of the country park. Never mind, we thought, it's lunch-time, so there will only be the one. At that moment another camouflaged monster flew even lower over our picnic-table, and *we* had to duck, stuffing our fingers into our ears so deeply it was difficult to get them out again.

Now, we are not quite sure whether it was the same two planes which terrorized us for the next hour, or whether sixty-four pilots had all been given instructions to make hell for human beings in search of heaven. As the sky grew noisier than any fury that the wrath of God might create on Judgement Day, we packed our belongings and headed for home. By this time I was suffering from such a persecution complex that I was wholly convinced that the fighters were after me, tracking me down, making me suffer for all my previous curses.

When, some days later, I voiced these feelings to a friend, whose husband is a pilot, she said, 'Ah, but remember! It's the price of freedom.'

I smiled briefly and said I had nothing against the pilots, only their machines. Would anyone, ever again, be able to write about 'the silence that is in the starry sky'?

And what, I wonder, would Rupert Brooke have to say about it all now. With what tone of voice would he ask: 'is there beauty yet to find?/And Certainty?/And Quiet kind?'

There is, alas, no certainty of beauty or quietness seventy

'Is there beauty yet to find? And Certainty? And Quiet kind?'

years after this question was asked. The uncertainty does, however, put a greater urgency on life to be lived to the full—and, as the late J. B. Priestley said shortly before his ninetieth birthday, 'Try to enjoy as much as you can.'

And so I lift myself out of the shades of despair, I emerge from the refuge of other people's thoughts and plan my excursion for tomorrow.

The fields wait
As they waited once for the first furrow
Or the first snow. They wait in silence
Under a generous sun. Between
Mist-fall and cock-crow,
Between rook-call and swallow,
They wait for the heart to respond,
For a new song to begin.

27 Chapel in the Mist

Little more than a Daley Thompson long-jump from the restless A47 is a sanctuary. It is not as well known yet as Little Gidding. Perhaps it is waiting for another T. S. Eliot to write a poem about it to guarantee such fame. It is roughly the same size as the small church where the Ferrar family worshipped in Huntingdonshire and, though less isolated, has the same feeling of remoteness.

The Puritan Chapel at Guyhirn, or Guyhirn Chapel of Ease as it is also known, is, nevertheless, a place of pilgrimage for anyone interested in the history of the Fens.

My own visit was made in privileged circumstances. Dr Peter Cave, who is Chairman of the Friends of Guyhirn Chapel of Ease, had invited me to meet him there on a late summer's afternoon so that I could learn more about the purpose of the building.

A million black corn midges decided to settle on us as we walked round the churchyard, which is still used for burials, and a couple of very low aircraft on bombing-practice again did their best to prove there was no such virtue as 'ease' left in the world today. Perhaps they were a convenient reminder that the world has always known troubled times and that this Puritan Chapel was itself a symbol of division and hope, of single-mindedness and belief.

A substantial part of the Chapel's history is speculative rather than documentative, because whatever records might have been kept have long since disappeared, being lost or destroyed. It is only through the dedicated research of people like Mrs M. B. Turner that we can piece together the many fragments which make up this compelling episode in our story.

With the Chairman's permission, I would like to make

Guyhirn Puritan Chapel

known the efforts of those who have made it possible for us to experience this unusual watershed of history, and I can do no better than repeat what you would find in the official guide, should you ever make your own pilgrimage:

> Guyhirn Puritan Chapel . . . is a small, plain, rectangular building situated in the village on the old Guyhirn-Wisbech road. A stone over the doorway records the date 1660 and the initials (of the builder or benefactor?) "R.P." However, whatever fascinating riddle the initials may present to the local historian, it is surely the date that is significant and which endears this little place with an importance out of all proportion to its size and location . . . The year 1660 was a turning-point unique in English history. It was the year in which England ceased to be a Commonwealth and reverted, following the death of Cromwell and the accession of Charles II, to what it had always been—a Monarchy . . .

Dr Cave spoke of how the church must have been built, using, no doubt, some of the stone from the ruins of

Thorney Abbey. The walls are partly brick and partly stone and give the impression of being constructed from whatever materials were freely available. As most of the Thorney stone had been sold to Cambridge University for the building of Trinity and Corpus Christi Colleges, and as this stone was transported by barge along the waterway which passed through Guyhirn (thanks to Bishop Morton), it is possible that a small quantity of it was unloaded for the Chapel.

I asked Dr Cave if he had any theories about the initials over the door.

'Only those which already exist. There was an influential family in the area by the name of Pearson, but I think it is more likely that the initials belong to Richard Pettigrew, who was a steward for the Bedford Estate at Thorney. His family had Puritan sympathies and he would have wished to help. Indeed, he may have been largely responsible for getting the Chapel built and would have deserved this kind of recognition.'

Despite, or because, of, its simplicity, the Chapel is a building of excellent proportions and looks perfectly at home on that strip of land between the Cambridgeshire and Lincolnshire Fens. I looked up at the bellcote and asked if it was the original one.

'We think so. The Chapel had a bellcote when it was built but the bell which is hanging there bears the initials "WW" and the date 1637, which is twenty-three years earlier than the date-stone above the door. It's believed that the bell may have come from the Puritan Chapel at Sandtoft in Yorkshire when the Huguenot refugees were driven south because of the religious persecution they were now finding in England. Several Huguenot/Walloon families settled in Thorney but, finding the Abbey there still pursuing "Popish practices" with its altar and high ritual, they would have sought a new refuge at Guyhirn. Many of them, of course, had strong Calvinist beliefs and would have wanted to establish their own meeting house for their particular style of worship.'

We stepped into the Chapel, and I was immediately struck by its lightness and austerity. There was no altar, only an old oak table and two chairs, a wooden lectern and a raised pulpit. There were no decorations or memorials. The walls were bare and the floor was of hand-made brick. I looked at the crude wooden hat-pegs which had once received the high-crowned hats of the period, and then at the bare pews, which looked as scrubbed and functional as butchers' chopping-tables used to be. They were stark in the extreme, with high backs and very narrow seats. It was difficult to appreciate how the Puritans could have sat on them for the two or three hours which their services often took, depending on the length of the preacher's sermon. The pews were also placed very close together to prohibit kneeling (which was held to be another 'Popish practice'), and the lack of all adornment in art or carving was meant to improve the worshippers' concentration on their prayers and the threatening words from the pulpit.

I stood for a few moments looking through the clear glass of the windows at the Fenland scene beyond. Thank goodness the Puritans also condemned stained glass, some of which can make a small church feel more like a mausoleum. From the remarkable serenity of that simple place I could see the afternoon light already beginning to fade. On the north side were the Lincolnshire Fens, and to the south were those of Cambridgeshire. Not far away was Crowland Abbey and, in other directions were those of Thorney and Peterborough. In their time they had lavished splendour and wealth on their buildings in praise of God. Here, in Guyhirn, was the complete opposite. Simplicity to the point of sparseness. Practicality reduced to the primitive. It could hardly have been called a 'chapel of ease' in Puritan times.

I turned from the window and sat in one of those hard pews, imagining myself as part of a congregation which would have assembled there three hundred years ago. There was a tense silence, an atmosphere which tingled with expectancy. I felt one with that community of men and women who had found in this place a refuge, a security, a meeting-place where, as T. S. Eliot said of Little Gidding, 'prayer has been valid'. But, as he continued, 'Prayer is more than an order of words . . . or the sound of the voice praying.'

I listened to the silence. And the silence had many voices.

In the absence of any documents before 1665, we can only trust what the silence has to say about Guyhirn and the people who worshipped there.

The Chapel is now maintained by the Redundant Churches Fund and cared for by the Friends of the Chapel of Ease. Why 'Chapel of Ease'? Because that was the name it was known by when it became a Chapel of Ease to Wisbech St Mary and the building was handed over to the Ely Diocese. Strangely, though, the Chapel has never been consecrated. The custom of consecrating and licensing churches was suspended during the Commonwealth, and Guyhirn remains singularly 'puritan'.

In 1960 the building was declared unsafe, and the last service was held on 5 November of that year. Inevitably a closed church quickly begins to deteriorate and become a ruin. Thirteen years of neglect meant that Guyhirn was nearing that state. But, fortunately, in 1973 a man appeared on the scene who was to change all that. The Reverend D. H. Dickinson had recently been appointed as the new incumbent of Wisbech St Mary's, and he soon called a meeting to see what could be done to restore the Chapel. As a result of that enquiry the Friends of Guyhirn came into being, and they, with the help of the Redundant Churches Fund, have made it not only a place of pilgrimage but also a place of worship once more. The annual Epiphany service is held each January and an annual Thanksgiving Service each July, with occasional services organized by the local school throughout the year. Plans for further use are being considered, but, in true Puritan tradition, there is no heating, no electric lighting and, with those very hard seats, no up-to-date comfort.

But do such things matter once in a while? Surely it is worth suffering a little hardship to enjoy the privilege of attending anything in a place like this—one of the few places of worship to have been built during another restless and uncertain period of history!

After more than ten years of hard work, and with nearly one hundred members, the Friends of Guyhirn should feel that all their efforts have been justified, their faith upheld, their hopes fulfilled.

As I left the quietness of that Chapel and drove away with Dr Cave to have tea in his lovely house on the North Brink at Wisbech, I knew that I had been in touch with more than history. I had felt something of Man's aspirations, doubts, desperations and needs. The fact that I had found this place in the Fens simply added to my existing depth of gratitude.

As I returned home, through Wisbech St Mary and Guyhirn, a silvery evening mist had put a bloom on the fields, the trees, the houses and the Chapel, which would always be surrounded by a mist of one sort or another.

28 From the Surgery to the Wishing Well, and Beyond . . .

When I met my friend Miss Audrey Fenney in Marks & Spencers one day and asked if she could find me one or two interesting Lincolnshire Fenmen to interview, I had no idea what I was letting myself in for. Perhaps I should have known better, because Audrey, who is a retired headmistress, still lives in the house and village where she lived as a child, and knows a lot of people in the area. Her family has been connected with farming for generations, and most of the land surrounding her house in Dyke is farmed by her cousin Philip Ash.

A few days after our chance meeting, the phone rang and Audrey was telling me of the programme she had worked out for me. It sounded a daunting task and, knowing how Fenmen can talk, I doubted if one day would be enough.

I arrived at her house on the edge of the village at 10.30 and, after a quick cup of coffee, was taken to meet Dr Alistair Galletly, a retired doctor of eighty-four who lives in Bourne. Dr Galletly, like his father before him, had spent all of his professional life caring for the sick in this part of Lincolnshire, which stretched from the uplands west of Edenham and Grimsthorpe to the eastern Fens as far as South Forty Foot. His 'parish' included Tongue End, Dyke Fen, Morton Fen, Haconby Fen and Dunsby Fen—and sometimes further afield in both directions.

'I had the best of both worlds, you see. On the one hand Bourne Woods and those beautiful stone villages around Grimsthorpe Park, and on the other, the great flat Fens and dreary hamlets bordering the drains . . . Have some sherry.'

'Did you prefer one to the other?'

'It all depended on what sort of mood I was in, and what the weather was like. When I was a young doctor, I did most of my country rounds on a bicycle, so I didn't care too much for the fog or the rain. But I loved the Fens in winter. I used to think there was nothing more exciting than watching that great red orb of the sun rising out of the snow and then, at the end of the day, to see it going down behind the bare trees of Bourne Woods. People forget that you can get some bright days in winter as well as grey ones. I think the winter light in the Fens is very special.'

'What else?'

'Moonlight! To see cornfields gently and silently waving under bright moonlight is quite thrilling. I used to enjoy those moments—the silvery light and the silence. I don't know anywhere else where you can get quite the same effect. The mist too could have its attraction. But not fog. I never liked the fog. Even on those straight Fen roads you felt pretty certain that you would end up in a dyke.'

'Did you find your Fenland patients difficult?'

'No worse than most. All patients can be difficult at times. It was difficult for us all fifty and sixty years ago. The death-rate was much higher when I started practising, because there were so many epidemics in the Fens then. The sanitation was unbelievably bad. Very often you would find fourteen people living in little more than a shack of one-up and one-down, and their only water supply was a communal tap shared by half a dozen families. The same with lavatories. The conditions were really quite appalling. It's a wonder there wasn't a revolution. Perhaps there should have been.'

'Were those people able to pay the medical bills?'

'If they were on the panel, they had assistance, of course. And if they couldn't always pay in cash, they would pay in kind. Very often we would have to wait until pig-killing time, but then they saw that we were all right. Occasionally a brace of pheasants would appear on the handle-bars of the bike. That sort of thing. They were honest people . . . Have some more sherry.'

'Have Fenland people changed very much?'

'People don't change. You will still find those who are as mean as muck and those who are very generous. Society

'Watching the great red orb of the sun beyond Bourne Woods'

has changed, and when people are taken out of their natural environment or relationships, they behave differently.'

'What about the National Health Service, which was introduced during your career? Did you welcome that?'

'Of course I did. Something had to be done to organize the business. It was getting out of hand. I thought it was a marvellous idea. Like a lot of other marvellous ideas, it has been abused by both patients and doctors alike, but in principle I agree with it.'

When I had arrived at Dr Galletly's house, I was invited in through the door which his patients had once used.

'I won't show you into the waiting-room,' he said, 'because it's a bit of a mess at the moment, but do come and see my old dispensary.'

I stepped into the small room still lined with shelves on which stood old medicine bottles, jars and various measures. Although the room had not been used for some years, the smells were still there, and my mind went back to the days of my childhood when I sat in the waiting-room of Dr Bernard's surgery in Whittlesey. We did not have chairs but long, narrow wooden forms, and the room always smelt of disinfectant and ancient copies of *Punch*. From where I sat I could just see, through the top half of the dispensary window, all its rows of blue bottles, brown jars and mysterious boxes, and I wondered from which ones would eventually be taken the potions for my own illness. It was not without some irony that I now saw myself on the other side of the wall.

Dr Galletly then led me through into the next room. 'And this was my consulting-room. This is where I heard about all their troubles. Where good news and bad news were exchanged, where I did my best to help the rich and the poor. In those days private patients had their medicines wrapped in white paper and sealed with red sealing-wax, which was a lot of bunkum. Panel patients had their medicines in whatever bottles they brought. I dread to think what might have been in some of them. Otherwise I tried to treat them all alike. Some private patients had been used to coming to the front door, but I did my best to discourage that custom, especially when there were twenty people or more queueing up at the surgery door. The only time I walked out of my surgery was when there was an emergency confinement which needed me.'

'When you have been the local doctor for so many years, you must feel very attached to the community!'

'Yes, you do. When you bring several children into the world for one family, you become part of their lives. When you bring hundreds of them into the world, you feel part of their whole existence. And when you see those children have their children, you begin to wonder how much longer you can go on being so involved. Of course it wasn't all joy. I used to get terribly upset if we lost the mother and saved the child. Things are much easier these days. When I was a young doctor, the only place where some of my patients could be sure of a clean bed was in the workhouse.'

From the consulting-room we had moved into an elegant drawing-room where we then sat and studied old Lincolnshire maps and continued to talk of the past.

'The one quality I have always noticed about the Fen people', said the doctor, 'was their resourcefulness. They never knew when they were beaten. They always found a way out of their problems. Very strong, very determined people. Salt of the earth . . . Sherry?'

I declined. I had to leave the doctor to his books, his memories and his lovely two-acre garden to make my way to the Wishing Well in Dyke, a village named after the Roman Car Dyke. Before leaving, I asked if he was optimistic or pessimistic about the future.

'All depends what sort of mood I'm in. I'd feel happier if the world could produce some decent leaders, but, if we don't do anything that's damned stupid, we should be all right. I hope so. It would be a pity if we spoilt it all now.'

The Wishing Well had been chosen as the most suitable and appropriate place for me to meet Ted Ash, Ben Laxton and Bill Packford—all locals and all willing to talk.

By the time I arrived, they were already half-way through their first round and were whetting their conversation on various aspects of village life from their early schooldays until their retirement. Although I had not met any of them before, I felt that I had just walked into a group of friends who had invited me to share their company.

Ted moved his rocking-chair closer to the wall to make room for me next to Bill, and the four of us crowded round the table like a group of conspirators. Within minutes the conversation had moved from the speed at which the harvest is gathered in these days to the way that young people amuse, or fail to amuse, themselves.

'They don't seem to appreciate the fields and the hedgerows like we used to,' said Ted. 'They were our amusement when we were kids.'

'And a lot of fun we used to have too,' Ben said, with a hint of the old mischief still in his eyes.

'When we were youngsters, the harvest used to last all summer. That's why the school holidays were so long. There was always something to do. Now there's no threshing or anything like that. It's all over in a week.'

'We used to go gleaning too. You never see that now. Do you remember going to the mill to get the corn ground?'

'And to the baker's on Sundays to get the joint cooked?'

All three men had lived in the village and had gone to the village school.

'You had to behave yourself too in them days, or you'd soon get a clip round the ear . . .'

'And another one when you got home if you told your mother.'

'Then there was Sunday School, every week, twice a day . . .'

'At least that got us on the Outings to Skegness . . .'

The Sunday School Outings kept them going for several minutes, and I then asked if the village had changed very much during their lifetime.

'Not that much . . . It's altered very little in a hundred years from what I've heard,' said Ted. 'If anything it's quieter now than what it was.'

'Why's that?'

They each offered a reason—fewer farm vehicles, fewer children, less social activity.

'The only noise we get these days is from visitors,' said Ben.

I apologized for my intrusion and bought them another round of drinks.

'You have to understand the nature of a village,' Bill explained. 'They're all different. I wouldn't want to live anywhere else, not now.'

'What about the Fens themselves?' I said. 'Do they mean anything to you?'

Ted, who had spent some time at sea, said, 'I used to say to people who didn't know this country that if you haven't travelled from Bourne to Boston by train you haven't seen England.'

Well, I thought, you can't better that, and for the next few minutes I listened to these true countrymen talking about the 'beauty of the evening skies', the 'glory of the Fens in every season', the 'quietness and the chance to be by yourself' and the 'feeling which you can't explain'.

'They can', as one of them said (and I was so taken by the statement that I failed to notice which one), 'always accommodate you.'

'It strikes me that you are all poets at heart.'

An embarrassed snigger ricocheted round the table. 'I doubt it!' said Bill. 'The only poetry I ever knew was at school, and I've long forgotten that.'

'Some of the old chaps in the village though were always rhyming about something or other, weren't they!' said Ben. 'Do you remember—

Mr Read has many apples
Which he sends away in crates.
He'll not need so many trays
To send away his 'tates' . . .?'

There were more tales and rhymes about the school-teacher, the chimney-sweep and the cobbler, anecdotes and memories of the characters who had sat in this pub sixty years ago, when it was called the Crown.

'There used to be an ale-house over the road, but you could never sit down in there.'

'Why not?'

'Ale-houses were only for standing. There was only one seat, and that was for the churchwarden. The rest stood. If you wanted to sit, you went to an inn. You'd never see a woman in an ale-house.'

I then asked them what they thought we have lost most in the country these days. Ted Ash had no hesitation in his reply: 'Husbandry. We've lost the art of husbandry.'

We had also lost track of time. The pumps had been closed and two hours had gone by without anyone hardly stopping for breath. I had forgotten about lunch and realized that I was much nearer my tea-time appointment with the Fenneys. The conversation was discontinued 'until another time'.

Fortunately Audrey managed to prepare a quick meal for me before her cousin Philip arrived to take me round part of the farm.

There were several questions I wanted to ask him, because, as a working farmer, he would be more interested in the problems of the present than the memories of the past.

As we drove over the sharp corn stubble left from the harvest, I asked about the ethics of stubble-burning.

'I know people who don't understand much about farming get very upset but it is the quickest and cleanest way of clearing the land. It's also good for the land. We just need to use a bit more common sense when it comes to burning. It's stupid if half a dozen farmers all decide to set light to their straw at the same time. Of course we're going to fill the sky with smoke and black ash which will fall on somebody's washing or wet paintwork. What we need to do is burn in rotation and consider the direction of the wind. If we don't control it ourselves, they will undoubtedly bring in further legislation and ban it altogether. Then we shall have a problem.'

Philip has, for many years, sat on the Black Sluice Drainage Board and is very interested in the problems of drainage, so I put the question to him that we might now be over-draining the Fens.

'I don't think so. I know there are those who think we do, but I believe we have got it right. Come over here and look at this drain . . .

We pulled up on the edge of a dyke where a small pumping-station controlled the water-level of that particular Fen. Considering the hot, dry summer, the water was surprisingly high, and, as Philip explained, they could not allow it to get any higher. He pointed to the uplands beyond Bourne Woods.

'You see, there's still a lot of water to come down from there, which we have to cope with down here. It's vitally important to keep the drains clean and the water-level under control.'

'But you can see quite a lot of dried-out dykes,' I said, 'dykes which have been neglected and are overgrown. What about those?'

'I agree. Some farmers don't bother, and the Internal Drainage Board has its difficulties. But, in principle, I think we are doing the right thing and draining correctly. After all, I wouldn't be doing anything to harm my own livelihood, would I!'

We crossed a dyke into a field of potatoes, and Philip stooped down to pull a couple of roots to show what a good crop there would be again this year.

'Feel that soil. Does that seem too dry or arid to you?'

I bent down and ran my hands through the soft earth, which felt damp, and the potatoes which I unearthed came out as cold as marble, their skins a smooth, unblemished red.

'What variety are these?'

'Desirée. They bake beautifully in their jackets. Would you like some?'

We gathered two or three roots and took them back to the car, then continued our tour of the farm.

'Crop-breeding has made such a difference to modern farming,' said Philip. 'We know what we take out of the soil and we know what needs putting back in. We know which seed to buy and which not, and can now make the land work for us all the year round without any problems. I have my soil analysed regularly, and the moment I find a deficiency, I put it right . . . It's not all take, you know. I've planted 250 trees this year, as I do most years. I also keep sheep, so I have to protect my pasture-land.'

'Are there many tied cottages left these days?'

'No. Farm workers prefer their own homes. I have a few cottages where old people live rent- and rate-free . . . I like to think that as a landowner I have a responsibility and that I meet it. I have a great admiration for these country people. They're kind, sensitive, reliable families . . . You would be surprised at some of the hobbies they have.'

I looked across the fields at some of the isolated farm labourers' semi-detached houses and thought of what a lonely existence it might be, especially during the long winter months. As we passed the end of one drove, I noticed a group of children playing on the dusty track.

'I wonder if they ever get to the sea!'

'Yes', said Philip, 'some do. I know of a voluntary organization which has sent twelve children to Skegness for a seaside holiday this year, all free.'

Now when Bill, Ted and Ben were children, I thought, they had to go to Sunday School to get a day at the sea . . . But there was no more time to ponder on all these different worlds within a world. My day at Dyke was over. We arrived back at Audrey's house, had a drink and then I made my way home.

The golden light of the evening had faded and the wispy clouds of sundown patterned the sky like pink Italian marble. My head ached, my voice was hoarse, my limbs were dowking. Dowking? Well yes! It was a new word I had just learnt and means, roughly speaking, wilting.

Perhaps I shall have to return to the Wishing Well for further refreshment before I can improve my vocabulary with any confidence. But that won't be for a little while, I fear.

29 Music of the Fens

As far as I know, the Fen country has not yet produced its own Sibelius to capture in sound our vast landscapes in the way that the Finnish composer did for his native land. The scope and scale of his music, I feel, get as near as any in evoking the lonely spaciousness and majesty of the Fens, and, although his symphonies are at the moment unfashionable, there is still a breadth and awesomeness about them which could have come out of the lowlands of East Anglia. But his music is not indigenous in the way that native music should be, and it is, therefore, only second-hand when I am looking for music to express the moods and character of my own landscape. Nor does his music finally have the 'quality of light' I would prefer.

All the ingredients and inspiration for such music are surely there in the Fens—the adagio-like movement of the wind through ripening corn, or the solemn larghetto-flow of a river in summer; the mysterious diminuendo of pylons into the distance or the pianissimo plainsong heard in the dykeside reeds. We could even add the dramatic crescendo of a winter sunrise or the Elgarian *nobilmente* of a glorious sunset; or the *cor anglais* cry of a solo pheasant.

All very fanciful, you may think! And why should I want to impose such a programme on anyone's music? Why not be content with the sad elegies to be heard on a winter's day in those bleak staves of telegraph wires which stretch across the fields? Why not be satisfied with the silent prelude and fugue of swallows and martins as they jostle like crotchets and quavers on the telephone wires outside my room? There are times when, as Keats said, 'Heard melodies are sweet, but those unheard/Are sweeter . . .'

Yet I must pursue this inquiry and ask, where is the

musical mind to translate all these natural wonders of the Fens into sound? Perhaps, if Benjamin Britten had lived in the heart of the Fens instead of Suffolk, his genius would have provided the answer. In place of those evocative 'Sea Interludes' from *Peter Grimes,* we might have had an opera on the 1947 floods, or a Fenland Cantata. As we know from 'The Curlew River', with its Fen setting, he understood the subtleties of such a sparse and mysterious landscape and could re-create the natural sounds of nature as well as anyone.

Somehow I don't think that Elgar would have been the man. He needed a more sumptuous countryside than we have to offer, and, although he is often referred to as 'the spirit of England', he surely needed the Malvern Hills and Worcestershire for his inspiration. Delius, for my taste, was always too romantic, and his impression of the Fens would have been over seductive. Ralph Vaughan Williams flirted with the Fenland Muse on at least one occasion, when, in 1907, he published his orchestral suite *In the Fen Country,* but it is seldom heard these days and is not encompassing enough to do the subject justice.

Like many composers who visited East Anglia, Vaughan

'Plaintive plainsong in the dykeside reeds'

Williams preferred Norfolk, though the composer I would choose for that county is the lesser-known E. J. Moeran, and it is regrettable that his music is not heard more often. In its quiet nostalgia it has a breath of that northern corner of East Anglia which is touchingly accurate.

A home-bred composer to emerge from Norfolk in the sixteenth century was John Wilbye, who was born at Diss and became one of the finest madrigalists the country has known. He later moved to Suffolk, where he was appointed Master of Music at Hengrave Hall, the home of Sir Thomas Kytson and family. This beautiful house still has a room known as the John Wilbye Room, and I have heard some of his music performed in that elegant setting.

During this century the counties bordering the Fens have generously provided home and inspiration for a number of composers, among them Gustav Holst, Michael Tippett, Benjamin Britten, Edmund Rubbra, William Alwyn, Malcolm Arnold and Trevor Hold. But the lowlands cannot, at present, match such illustrious names as those which have already brought distinction to Essex, Norfolk, Suffolk and Northamptonshire.

Understandably much of the music which has come from the Fen country has been sacred rather than secular. Our abbeys have always been renowned for their good singing, even from those early days when King Canute heard the monks of Ely and was so impressed that he ordered his oarsmen to row closer to the bank so that he could hear more clearly.

> Merily sang they, the monks at Ely,
> When Canute the King he rowed thereby:
> Row to the shore, men, said the King,
> And let us hear these monks to sing.

An Isle of Ely man who has kept his name firmly in the annals of Church music is Christopher Tye, who will be remembered as the composer of 'While Shepherds watched their flocks', if nothing else. After training as a chorister at King's College, Cambridge, he became a lay clerk at Ely, where, in 1541, he was appointed Master of Music. During his years there he composed several masses, motets and anthems, some of which are still performed in our cathedrals today. He was followed by Robert White (1561) and John Anmer (1579-1641), who, according to Groves, 'wrote much fine music' which has only recently been published.

Ely has maintained its tradition of both making and creating 'fine music' through its present Master of Music, Dr Arthur Wills, who has so far composed over one hundred pieces, including many excellent organ works and a symphonic suite for organ and brass band, called *The Fenlands*—a substantial contribution to the area's music.

If I include Cambridge in this survey—and the city is, after all, a cornerstone of the Fens—I immediately gather in a few more riches, such as John Dowland, Orlando Gibbons and W. Sterndale Bennett. But the most local and interesting of musicians to represent Cambridge must be Patrick Hadley, who was born there in 1899 and died in King's Lynn in 1973. Among his many compositions was *Fen and Flood,* originally written for men's voices and first performed in June 1955.

Barry Ferguson, though a Devon man (and now Master of Music at Rochester), was educated at Cambridge and later became assistant organist to Dr Stanley Vann at Peterborough Cathedral. In 1972 I had the privilege of collaborating with him on his *Katharine of Aragon Cantata* which had been commissioned by the *Peterborough Standard* for performance in the cathedral. In the bleak, echoing and spacious setting of 'The cold mist of autumn haunts the Great Fen', Ferguson caught exactly the mood of the landscape as I know it at that late time of the year and, equally, as the exiled Catherine must have known it before the Fens were drained. The xylophone introduction alone sends a Fenland shiver down the spine.

Staying with Peterborough Cathedral for a moment, I usually take pleasure in pointing out to visitors that the first organist there was Richard Storey (1540), but whether I can claim him as an ancestor or not I do not know. Since his entry on that roll of honour there have been several distinguished organist/composers, including John Mudd (1584) and Thomas Mudd (1631). Dr Haydn Keeton (1870) wrote a few anthems, but his chief contribution to music generally must be through two of his very distinguished young pupils: Sir Malcolm Sargent and Sir Thomas Armstrong. Stanley Vann recalled for me recently how Sir Malcolm had said, just a few years before his death, that he owed everything (musically) to Dr Keeton and Peterborough Cathedral. 'He was', said Dr Vann, 'very moved when he came to the cathedral with the BBC Symphony Orchestra and played the organ again. He had not seen the new 1930 console on the south side—it was on the north side in his days—and he was almost in tears as he came down from the loft.'

Dr Vann himself was a very fine choir-trainer and arranger, whose only standard was perfection. He too has composed and published several anthems, services and carols—an activity which he continues in retirement and one which will add further distinction to his considerable achievements.

A recent composition associated with the cathedral is Trevor Hold's dramatic choral work *Old Scarlett*—the story of the sexton Robert Scarlett who, in addition to burying Catherine of Aragon and Mary, Queen of Scots, also claimed to have buried the dead of Peterborough twice over. As my libretto had him say:

I buried the fathers, I buried the sons.
Two generations, one after the other.
And many times I have had to throw
Out the bones of one for another.
For the churchyard was full
And the graves were bespoke,
And the child often followed its mother.

Sometimes my spade would hit the skull
Of a neighbour or his brother,
And then I would coax them gently
To make room for one another.
When the churchyard was full
I would say to them all
'Come on, my friends, move over!'

Before leaving Peterborough, mention must be made of

James Blades, the internationally famous percussionist, who was born in the city. He has played with all the major orchestras of the world and, in later years, he lectured most entertainingly on his profession.

Further north, from the Lincolnshire Fens, came a man who was considered to be one of the greatest English composers of the Tudor period—John Taverner, who was born near Boston in 1490 and died there in 1545. Throughout his early career he composed a great amount of music for the Catholic Church but during the Reformation became converted to the Protestant cause and, as one music critic said of him, 'lost his artistic soul as a result of these events'. Not only was he a composer himself but he has been the source of music in others, for a few years ago Peter Maxwell Davies composed an opera based on the earlier man's life.

And still, with all this, you ask, I still look for a Sibelius, Mahler, Bruckner or Fauré? I have the uneasy feeling that by the time this is printed someone will have told me that I have overlooked such a talent. If so, I apologize in advance and offer to lead the applause.

In the meantime it is to Nature that I must return to hear the kind of music which I think should come from the Fenland fields. And where would I be but on some high riverbank with the silent waters at my feet and a hundred thousand acres within my sight, waiting for those almost inaudible sounds which echo across the earth and, like divine music, send a shiver down the spine. Or maybe I would choose to be somewhere at night, on a lonely road or leaning on a five-barred gate, listening to the unheard music of the stars, or to those ancient voices of men who sang here long ago. And, if music *is* most effective through the silences it creates, then I would listen to the silence and know that I stood in the presence of some great Master.

30 A Day of Reckoning

The land looked resigned to winter. Those fields which had grown cereals were already cleared and ploughed ready for next year's crops. There were still a few acres of celery to be lifted and a field or two of carrots, but they would probably never be lifted at all. It was a quiet, elegiac morning. Most of the seasonal birds had gone, and I thought of Eric Slote in nearby Ramsey St Mary, who had said to me, 'The migration of birds is my calendar. They govern my seasons.' There was a feeling of emptiness rather than fulfilment. The year would all too soon be over.

Perhaps my own mood had been conditioned by seeing a funeral cortège making its way across those Fenland roads, either to the church in Yaxley or to the crematorium in Peterborough. The shiny hearse and three other cars passed by slowly, yet they were there for no more than a few seconds before their brief moment of grief was swallowed up in eternity and the reality of it registered with me. Someone who had known and loved these Fens would see them no more. The bright splash of flowers on the coffin, the sad faces of the mourners, the dead and the living, were there one moment, and the next had vanished. The last time I had spent a morning out in Holme Fen, it was early spring. Over the fields lay an almost imperceptible mist like the bloom on black grapes. The land was freckled with countless pieces of carrot, remnants of last year's unwanted crops which had been ploughed in because there was no market for them.

I had stopped to look at the field more closely when a man and his dog appeared from nowhere. The man was, perhaps, in his late seventies and wore thick, grey woollen trousers and a black jacket. Small, bright eyes shone from

'Stopping to look at a field more closely'

his lined face. They were Fenmen's eyes—fierce, cautious, questioning. His black labrador looked as old, but its eyes were misty with age, and its coat was threadbare.

'You lookin' for somethin'?'

'No. Just wondering why all those lovely carrots had to be ploughed in.'

'Cus nobody wanted them. It's a rum old world when we have to plough back into the land half of what we grow. But that's how it is.'

'Couldn't the farmer have given them away?'

'Don't make me laugh. Farming's not about giving. It's all taking, especially with these Common Market subsidies. It pays 'em to be over-productive. It's the same with milk, with dairy cattle. When I started working on the land sixty year ago, there were no such things as butter mountains or milk lakes. We had to work hard to make the land pay. We didn't get any Government hand-outs.'

'You've seen a few changes then!'

'You could say. I've known nothin' else but land work, but I doubt if I'd enjoy it any more. In any case they don't need men now, it's all machines. The last farm I worked on employed seventy men. Now there are two.'

'And yet we over-produce.'

'Of course. It pays to over-produce. Grow the bloody stuff and then plough it back, or pour it down the drain, what does it matter? I think it's an insult to nature. And if we don't plough it in, what do we do with it? Give it to the Russians or the Arabs. There'll be a day of reckoning, you mark my words.'

The black labrador had wandered off into the field, and in the distance a 125 high-speed train swished along the skyline between King's Cross and Peterborough.

'How would you change things?' I asked.

'Don't ask me. I'd do away with committees to start with. They never get anything done. And I'd do away with the Common Market if I had my way. We should have never sold out on our Commonwealth countries. When we were fighting the war, we needed them to help us. The moment it's all over, we tell 'em to get lost. It seems a poor way of showing our gratitude, if you ask me. But then, I don't understand things any more.'

We walked for a short distance along the grass verge and came to a lorry-load of rubbish that had recently been dumped there.

'You see what I mean? That never used to happen. People had respect for the countryside. Now they think it's somewhere to chuck all the rubbish they don't want. Somebody else's got to clear that up. That's not necessity or thoughtlessness. That's barbarism for which there should be a £500 penalty. Personally I'd put the buggers up against the wall and shoot 'em.'

A mattress and an old armchair had fallen into the dyke. Cans, bottles and the remains of a child's cot stuck out grotesquely from the rest of the litter. The man had every right to be angry, as I was, and as every farmer, land-owner or rural council should be. It is an eyesore one sees far too frequently, and the offenders should be heavily fined, if only they could be caught.

I thought of what Michael Stagg, the Warden of the Suffolk Heritage Coast, had said to me earlier in the year when he likened himself to King Canute. 'We are trying to turn back the tide of pollution, destruction and apathy. And apathy is the most difficult one of all.'

We understandably get angry and alarmed when we hear of heathlands and ancient meadows being ploughed up—and over eighty per cent of our heathlands and forty per cent of our meadows have been lost so far this century—but there are other vandals at work, and the countryside is under greater threat than it has ever been before. In our careless ways we abuse the natural beauty around us all the time. Whether heathlands are destroyed by fire or the plough, they are lost forever and with them a whole, intricate world of wildlife is sacrificed. A two-hundred-year-old tree, cut down because it was in someone's way, cannot be replaced overnight. Nor can heaths or meadows, which have existed since the Middle Ages, ever be reclaimed once they have gone. It is disturbing when we read in the national Press that 126,000 miles of hedgerow have been destroyed in this country during the last thirty years and that more than a third of our grazing land has gone under the plough.

Having aired our grievances and having accepted the fact that we could do little to change the course of the world, the man and I parted company. As I made my way back to the car, he went off to look for his dog. 'Nelson! Nelson!', I heard him calling over the field; a true and thorough Englishman who couldn't 'understand things any more'.

I made my way towards Ramsey St Mary, Ramsey Heights and Wood Walton Fen, that sanctuary of peace and solitude, of calm and restoration—a place of old, rare, sweet smells which can be found nowhere else. The scent of the black earth, the water, reed, grass, wild flowers, meadow-sweet, lady's smock, white campion, hemp, agrimony, wild rose and weeds, heavy with dew. Whenever you go, whatever the season, there is always something to remember. You feel that the air you breathe in Wood Walton Fen has never been near pollution, never heard an unmusical sound or received an unwanted smell. It emanates from the earth as from the beginning of time. It would make a suitable setting for Eden. Everything about it has a touch of the newly created, or, rather, of the innocent and unspoilt. I would like to believe that, if I were able to return to earth in a hundred years time, that Fen would be just the same. But, to resume my mournful mood, that is perhaps being over-optimistic. Eden happens only once in a lifetime.

Now it is autumn and I am thinking more of spring, remembering a morning which already seems a century away. A new mist creeps over the land and into the trees. I pause at the place where I stood talking to the man and look to see if the dog is still sniffing about in the field. The field is empty. The man already part of the past.

Which way shall I go now? How indecisive we can be when the time is so short! I remember what Thoreau said: 'To kill time is to injure eternity.' But I'm not always sure when I am killing time or when I am waiting for something to happen. One has to learn how to wait. Most of my best writing moments have come when least expected, when I have had the patience to sit still and wait. At the same time I could not sit there forever. I had to decide which way to go.

Eventually I went to Ramsey St Mary and turned left towards Whittlesey. In the distance I could see the impressive spire of St Mary's church and appreciated, perhaps for the first time, why it was often selected by other travel-writers as one of the finest spires in the Fens. Because I had known it all my life, I had accepted it as just another spire, but in the clear light of an autumn morning it stood out on the skyline like the mast of a great ship that had just returned from a voyage round the world.

Even the simple act of driving towards my home-town gave a purpose to the day. My end was at my beginning. I was returning. These were the roads I had cycled on as a boy. These were the dykes where I had gathered reed-mace and collected frog-spawn for school. Soon there was the river where I had picked wild irises and tried to catch fish. There was the church of St Andrew and the Briggate Bridge, from which James Spencer's father had fallen and broken his neck. There was the Boat public house where Pete Morgan had been 'bowled over' by Whittlesey and its people.

How fortunate I had been to grow up in this funny, ordinary, sometimes ugly, fascinating, independent and proud little town. Perhaps it was time to take stock again, to have my own day of reckoning. As I drove down the street where I was born, I felt a strange, tingling excitement, that compelling sense of 'belonging' which will not let us go.

There are, occasionally, times when I wish I could have been born more in the heart of the Fens instead of on the periphery, but the avantage of living on the edge of things is that one can usually be a better observer. I have always had to journey into the interior, and the travelling has been half the fun. Not that I felt in those early years that I was in any way on the outside of life in the Fens. Whittlesey in those days was a much more independent place than it is today. In an age when county boundaries were not as meaningless as they are now, Peterborough was a foreign country, and I belonged very much to the Isle of Ely. The people, too, were without question 'Fenland people' who had come up into the town from the Fens and who still had all the characteristics of the old breed of Fenmen. Some of the old families, of course, are still there and retain those qualities I have already described. But I fear their days are numbered. It is getting harder now to find the true spirit of the Fens, both in the people and in the places, unless you know of somewhere like the George and Dragon at Littleport or can be alone on some remote dykeside when the mist has erased the horizon and you stand in a no-man's-land where there are no boundaries, no loud intrusions from the world outside, only the silent awareness that once this was a kingdom where individuals valued their freedom above all things and where, for the time being, nature has finally surrendered her wrath to the demands of Man. The next drama may not be of nature's making.

31 Last of the Tribe?

'For better for worse, for richer for poorer'–we don't hear these traditional words of the Marriage Service repeated so often these days, like much else which has been lost from the Book of Common Prayer.

I heard them again at a friend's wedding, which took place in a small church on the edge of the Fens one Saturday afternoon towards the end of harvest, and thought them appropriate for the opening sentence of this last chapter.

When I started this book at the beginning of the year, I really had no idea what it would contain, what sort of crop it would yield by the time of its completion. But here I am, on the last few pages, and I have been surprised on more than one occasion by what has come my way.

And now, at the end of another season and another journey into the Fens, I have to ask myself, 'What have I learnt this time? What has this long marriage between a land and its people been able to prove?'

To begin with, I wanted simply to praise, to say again what a splendid and inadequately appreciated countryside it is; but it is not as easy and as uncomplicated as that. What I have come to realize is that we all live in a privileged but extravagant, selfish and changing world which has not left the Fens untouched.

In 1984 twenty-two million tons of grain were grown in England, and most of it went to join the already existing 'grain mountain' of the EEC—along with the other mountains of butter, barley and beef and the lakes of milk and wine. It will cost the EEC something like £1,800 million just to store this harvest which is surplus to our requirements. During the same year 500,000 head of cattle and 100,000 people died in Africa through lack of food and water. One gets the feeling that something is wrong somewhere!

So why, you may ask, do I go into ecstatic rhapsodies about a countryside and an industry which can only add to our embarrassment, if, indeed, it is embarrassment we feel? I do not know the answer, when I am faced with such statistics. They are part of a year, part of a world, and what I have written about is but a small fragment of the whole.

All the people, places, achievements and failures exist, and have happened, within fifty miles of where I live. Yet, so diversified and extreme have been the views and experiences of the men and women with whom I talked that I cannot believe they have all belonged to one nation, let alone one area. I feel as if I have travelled half-way round the world instead of just five thousand miles around the Fens.

But this much did emerge—individuals may vary in their backgrounds and beliefs, yet they can still be held together by a common love of place, giving to airy nothing 'a local habitation and a name'. All their attitudes and peculiarities can be united into one specific character.

Whether I spoke with people who had known nothing but hard work on the land or with those who had achieved success by using different energies and skills, I felt there was a common denominator. It was more than nostalgia, more than a sentimental longing for those 'good old days' which never were, more even than a loyalty to the place which had, for one reason or another, become home. It was a recognition of a tradition, of belonging to a tribe that had somehow survived longer than most.

Even this does not fully explain the 'spirit of the Fens' I set out to find. It makes those people sound no more than the survivors of a parochialism which some social reformers would say is unhealthy, as if, in belonging to a place, there lurked the sinister seeds of nationalism.

There were no signs of such evils among the people I met, and I am sure that healthy parochialism can be found anywhere in the country. What I discovered transcends the parish pump and the reorganized county boundaries. It was an identity with history and a stubborn resistance to anything in the present which tries to obliterate the past, just for the sake of change.

But is there any virtue in defying change, any virtue in not conforming or being manipulated by modern society? How long, I wonder, will these defiant, stubborn, independent descendants of the marsh-dwellers survive? And when they've gone, shall we miss them? And what, in the end, will bring about the demise of such a tribe?

I can make no prophecy or answer any of these questions. Change comes about in the most unexpected and often most innocent of ways. When I asked one of my octogenarian friends what he thought had been the greatest change in the Fens, he said, 'Roads.'

'It all began with the roads. Roads and bridges. When I were a boy, eighty years ago, you couldn't travel about the Fens like you can today. When you went to work on a farm, you stayed there. You had no choice in winter. There were no roads to go from one place to another. No bridges over the rivers or the dykes, unless you were prepared to walk twenty miles out of your way. People lived in tied cottages then and had to make their own entertainment. That's what made them such good story-tellers. That and the beer. There were no television or radio. If you were lucky enough to get to a pub in them days, you would always find someone who could keep the night going with a few good yarns. I used to go to a place called the Three Fishes. That's not there now but when I was a young-un you could sit there all night with a pint of beer and a packet of Woodbines for a tanner . . . A lot has happened in a hundred years—motor-cars, air travel, men on the moon, heart-transplants, you name it. I tell you, if our old grandparents could come back now, they'd think the world had gone mad.'

'But, surely, they would quickly learn to accept and come to appreciate the benefits of our technological age, just as we have done?'

'I doubt it. I believe a man belongs to a certain time. He can't go back and he can't go forward. I'm pretty certain that my parents wouldn't want to live now, not after being brought up in the world they knew, and I'm equally certain that I wouldn't want to live in the world in fifty years time, not the way it's going. I've had my time.'

So are the people who I have been writing about really the last of their tribe? Is the traditional Fenman a thing of the past, a dodo or a bog-oak, to be resurrected from age to age only for other people's curiosity? I don't think so. Something inherent in the nature of the Fenman will survive. The character of a people which has questioned every development since William the Conqueror, which has defied all the threats of nature herself, will surely not perish so easily.

It should also be remembered that this single-mindedness is not simply one-eyed blindness or resistance to progress. Fenmen are not defiant just for the hell of it. Some of the most advanced methods of agriculture in the world and some of the greatest technological achievements have been pioneered in the Fens.

The point, I feel, has been made. I have established, for my own satisfaction at least, that the 'spirit of the Fens' is not a figment of my imagination, and the native Fenman is not yet a myth. Both exist and both are healthy.

In the end it all comes down to something very personal anyway. During the writing of this book I have learned far more about the Fen country than I knew, and my love for it has deepened because of this latest intimacy. I have met many people I had not met before, and several of them have added rich layers of friendship to those already possessed. And this I must say again, that when a Fenman eventually offers friendship, it is his bond and he will mean it to last. He hates to be forgotten, ignored or let down.

My last words, however, must be for the land itself, for that is the mother of us all who feel that we are 'expressions of the soil'. Having reached this point, I still cannot say which is my favourite place, which is my favourite season or time of day in the Fens. There have been moments at every swing of the sun's pendulum which I could select as the one moment I would remember above all others. But the moment that choice is made, another nudges itself into second place.

If I were ever marooned on a desert island or imprisoned in a city, I would long for a late August day on the edge of a harvest field which had just been cut. That beach of golden stubble would be far more attractive to me than a Pacific shore. If ever I found myself stranded near the earth's equator, I am sure I would pine for a misty morning in November, when stillness is as visible as cob-webs on hedges, or console myself with the memory of an April morning on a dykeside near Welney under a sky full of larks.

It is the mood which is important, and any season or view which can offer me an expansive moment of peace, or visual excitement, gets my vote. It could be a mild June evening when the low light of the sun varnishes the land, making the new green shoots glow as though lit from within. It could be a quiet summer's afternoon when there is a lull between farming activities, and a soft breeze teases the earth with nothing better to do than wait. Or it could be a late autumn day when the fields are empty, the birds' songs ended and the first hint of winter is seen in the stiffening waters of the dykes. As long as there were those essential qualities of light, space, distance and something approaching silence, then I would be content, whatever the season or the hour of day.

This year the storehouse is full enough to keep me happy for the next twelve months, if not a lifetime. I can look back on a year in which I have enjoyed conversations with people as diverse as Hugh Cave, Henry Beusch, Eric Slote, John Bennett, Dr Galletly, Henry Dean, Arthur Turner, George Ellingham, Bertram Winterton, Steve Wesley and many others. What a roll-call! What a delightful way to spend a year! I have sat in simple cottages and elegant rooms, have walked the headlands and bounced across ploughed fields in Range-Rovers and tractors, listening for hours to people talking about what the Fens mean to them. I feel embarrassed to call it 'work'.

But, even in such a full and generous year, I realize that I have again only scratched at the surface of this very individual world. There are many parts of the Fens which I have not described, many places which I have not written specifically about for the purpose of this book. I think of a town like March, for instance, through which I frequently passed on my way to somewhere else but which receives no more than a few references in these pages. Such an omission is not meant in any way to be a snub or to suggest a lack of interest. March, too, in its own way evokes a 'spirit of the Fens' and has been important in the making of our history. One day, perhaps, when I need to write again about this

'The rest cannot be written'

area, it will feature with others in my jubilation at discovering something new about a landscape which is always full of surprises.

Paths have a happy knack of crossing at the right moments, and people come into one's life at the most propitious time. I would be saddened if I thought that there was nothing left to discover, no one else waiting to share with me part of their own enthusiasm and loyalty for the Fens. But, for now, I must be satisfied with what the year has given—the sweet, the sour, the hollow and the whole. Next year will have other gifts to offer, as W. H. Auden wrote, 'Another time has other lives to live.'

Finally, at the end of it all, I am made even more aware of the truth of the words by F. S. Smythe which I quoted in my introduction: 'Words at their best can only reveal a quality; they cannot do more than present a glimmering . . .'

Here, then, for better for worse, is a glimmering of the beauty, pleasure, enlightenment and company which I have experienced in searching for the spirit of the Fens. For richer for poorer, these words have to suffice. The rest cannot be written.

Index